# MY MISSION IS TO
# SPREAD HAPPINESS

## Sai Baba's teachings

### A LIST OF SAI BABA'S TEACHINGS
### WITHOUT SANSKRIT WORDS

DIANA LEWIS

# MY MISSION IS TO SPREAD HAPPINESS

*Sai Baba's teachings*

**A LIST OF SAI BABA'S TEACHINGS
WITHOUT SANSKRIT WORDS**

**MEREO**

Cirencester

## Published by Mereo

Mereo is an imprint of Memoirs Publishing

25 Market Place, Cirencester, Gloucestershire, GL7 2NX
info@memoirsbooks.co.uk  www.memoirspublishing.com

### My mission is to spread happiness
#### Sai Baba's teachings

ISBN: 978-1-86151-012-9

# INTRODUCTION

I first heard about Sai Baba when I attended the local Meditation Group where I live in Somerset, England. The group was run by a very spiritual couple named Bill and Tessa Armstrong in the year of 1992. During one of their evenings they showed a short film of Sai Baba walking in amongst his devotees taking letters from them and speaking with them in his Ashram known as Prasanthi Nilayam. I was struck by the look of devotion on the devotees' faces and thought that Sai Baba must be a very special person indeed.

Ten months later Sai Baba started to come into my dreams, and also at this time I was aware of the fragrance of jasmine in my home and of his presence there. As I have always believed in the existence of God and have a connection with Him. I asked Him through telepathic thought if He was in the body of Sai Baba and He said 'Yes, Yes, Yes!'

My first journey to see Sai Baba was not until January 1997 but what a divine, loving experience that was! Sai Baba gave me so much love. He proved to me without a shadow of a doubt that He was my best friend, God, in human form. I have been lucky enough to visit Sai Baba five times since that time and each time I see Him I am filled with His love and bliss.

No one can really introduce Sai Baba, but the little that I know of him I have written below:

Sai Baba was born on the 23rd November 1926 in a small village called Puttaparthi, in Andhra Pradesh, India. His earthly mother was Easwaramma and His earthly father was Pedda Venkapa Raju. Sai Baba has had an Ashram built in the village of Puttaparthi which has accommodation, a library, a book centre, a supermarket and bank, three canteens for various tastes and many other facilities. He has called the ashram "Prashanti Nilayam", meaning the "Abode of the Highest Peace." He has transformed this unknown village of Puttaparthi into a thriving Spiritual Centre where many people from all over the world visit Him to receive His Divine blessings and listen to His sacred spiritual teachings.

Sai Baba has inaugurated the Sri Sathya Sai Institute of Higher Medical Sciences known as the Super Speciality Hospital situated in Prasanthigram, near Puttaparthi, which has the latest medical technology for treating many ailments. There are eight operating theatres, two for cardiology, three for ophthalmology and three for urology. The construction of 15,000 square metres with ultra modern facilities took one year to construct. There is another Super Speciality Hospital situated in Whitefield, Bangalore, again with all modern facilities.

All medication is free of charge. Sai Baba says "In life, health is the greatest wealth".

In Puttaparthi, Sai Baba has inaugurated the building of the Institute of Higher Learning (a University), Primary Schools, a Planetarium, a Sports Centre, a large Super Speciality Hospital, a smaller hospital, two Museums (showing all the different faiths) and a Music College. All education is also free of charge.

He has also inaugurated the building of the Sri Sathya Sai Arts and Science College for women in Anantapur, and a Sri Sathya Sai Arts and a Science College for men in Brindavan in Bangalore.

Sai Baba has formed The Sathya Sai Organisation. The organisation is not for a religion and is non-profit making. It is open to all faiths to congregate in unity to learn and put into practise Sai Baba's spiritual teachings.

Sai Baba's services to the local people include the digging-out of wells and canals so that much-needed water could be supplied to many villages and towns such as Chennai in India. He has sent His service team of willing volunteers out to many other countries to rescue, feed and generally help in areas where help of every sort is urgently needed. Also He feeds the poor and distributes clothes for them. Sai Baba has also constructed a home for orphan children near Puttaparthi, where they are provided with food, clothing and an education so that they are able to lead a life of honour and dignity.

Sai Baba gives unconditional love and selfless service all day long – every day! He has generated a long list of service to humanity and the animal kingdoms during his life time and He says 'My Mission is to Spread Happiness. I do not take anything from anyone, except their Love and Devotion'.

Sai Baba's full name is Bhagavan Sri Sathya Sai Baba and He is what is known as an 'Avatar'. An Avatar is a Divine Incarnation, in other words God has taken on a human body. He has come to re-establish divine knowledge known as the Vedas. The Vedas are God's universal laws and were communicated by God to holy men that were living in India in ancient times. Sai Baba has come to teach us of the Vedic Truth of humanity's inherent divinity and also to re-educate us in the five Human Values of Love, Truth, Right Action, Non-Violence and Peace. He is the Avatar of this age who has come to lead humanity back on to the Spiritual Path by teaching who we really are, where we have come from and why we are here.

He teaches that the principles of Truth, Righteousness, Peace, Equanimity and Selfless Love should govern all human relations and activities.

Sai Baba has come to help us. He says "His life is His message".

The reason I have written this book is because I feel there is a great need for Sai Baba's teachings to be known in the rest of the world. I hope that by reading this book and by accepting this divine truth He has come to give us, people will change towards each other by becoming more loving and caring and hopefully make the world a happier and better place to live in.

A monthly magazine called the Sanathana Sararthi is published at Prasanthi Nilayam which contains Sai Baba's teachings taken from his various discourses. Within this book I have copied most of these teachings from these magazines but some have been copied from other sources.

**I dedicate this book to my best friend, Sai Baba**

# CONTENTS

# SAI BABA - THE AVATAR
## (GOD IN HUMAN FORM)

Sai Baba has said 'For the protection of the virtuous, for the destruction of evil-doers and for establishing righteousness on a firm footing, I incarnate from age to age. Whenever disharmony overwhelms the world, the Lord will incarnate in human form to establish the modes of earning peace and to re-educate the human community in the paths of peace. At the present time, strife and discord have robbed peace and unity from the family, the school, society, the religions, the cities and the state. The arrival of the Lord is also anxiously awaited by saints and sages. Spiritual aspirants prayed and I have come.

As the vapour of the clouds form droplets and fall upon the fields they choose to foster, the "Formless Absolute" individualizes "itself", assumes a form and comes down among humanity to save and sustain it.

Every step in the career of the Avatar is predetermined. When people forget the One and run after the many, righteousness declines; and there can be no love, no sacrifice, no detachment in human affairs. So the Lord takes human form and comes amongst men to restore their sense of values.

In this human form of Sai, every divine entity, every divine principle, that is to say all the names and forms ascribed to God by man, is manifest. My power is immeasurable. My truth is inexplicable, unfathomable. There is nothing I do not see, nowhere I do not know the way, no problem that I cannot solve. **I am the totality – all of it.**

I am Omnipresent (everywhere); I am Omnipotent (all powerful) and I am Omniscient (all seeing). I do not come and go. I am everywhere present, at all times. Do not waste your capacity trying to understand Me. It is beyond anyone's capacity to understand Me. It is only when you succeed in knowing yourself that you can know Me.

My Mission is to spread Happiness. I do not take anything from anyone, except their Love and Devotion. Be near, watch, learn and believe in Me.

I live in the experience that I am one with everyone. My love flows out to all and I see everyone as Myself. If a person reciprocates My love from the depths of his heart, My love and his love meet in unison and he is cured and transformed.

See in Me yourself, for I see Myself in all of you. You are My life, My breath, My soul. When I love you, I love Myself. When you love yourselves, you love Me!

I have separated Myself from Myself, so that I may love Myself. My beloved ones, you are My Own Self!

You are as close to God as you are to yourself.

Wherever you walk, I am there. Whomsoever you contact, I

am in that person. I am in each. From each I will respond. You cannot see Me in one place and miss Me in another, for I fill *all* space. You cannot escape Me or do anything in secret. Wherever and whenever you think of Me, I shall be with you. Whenever you call to Me, I shall respond.

Come just one step forward and I shall take a hundred towards you. Shed just one tear and I shall wipe a hundred from your eyes. My hand always gives, it never takes.

I must tell you that total adherence to truth – absolute selflessness – universality and spontaneous outpouring of love are to be seen in Sai and nowhere else.

The world is the creation of God. Right from man, all living beings including animals, birds and even insects are the creation of God. Since they are the creation of God, all of them have their origin in bliss.

You must have freedom not only from fear, but from hope and expectation. Trust in My wisdom. I do not make mistakes. Love My uncertainty for it is not a mistake. It is My intent and will. I will grant you what you need and deserve; there is no need to ask, no reason to grumble. Be content; be grateful, for whatever happens, whenever it happens. Nothing can happen against My Will.

Why fear when I am here? Put all your faith in me, and I shall guide and guard you.

I do not appreciate in the least the distinction between the various appearances of God, Sai, Rama, Krishna, Jehovah, Allah, etc. I do not proclaim that one is more important than the others. Continue your worship of your chosen God along the lines already familiar to you. Then you will find that you are coming nearer and nearer to Me for all names and all forms are Mine. There is only <u>one God</u> and He is Omnipresent.

Each religion forgets that God is ALL Forms and ALL Names. There is only ONE religion and that is the Religion of Love.

Believe that all hearts are motivated by the One and Only God. That all faiths glorify the One and Only God. That all names in all languages and all forms man can conceive – denote the One and Only God. Cultivate the attitude of Oneness between men of all creeds, all countries and all continents. That is the Message of Love I bring. That is the Message I wish you to take to heart.

I am a child amongst children, a student amongst students, a woman amongst women, a man amongst men, and God when I am by Myself. Approach Me without fear as a right.

You may be seeing Me today for the first time but you are all old acquaintances of mine; I know you all through and through.

I will never desert you or deny you, or turn away from you. I am the nearest, the dearest, the most loving, the most eager, companion, comrade and kinsman for Man.

You must dive deep into the sea to get the pearls. What good is it to dabble amongst the waves near the shore, and swear that the sea has no pearls in it and that all tales about them are false? So also, if you must realise the full fruit of the Avatar, dive deep and get immersed in Me.

Everyone has to be asked to approach me and experience me. In order to get an idea of a mountain, it is not enough if you show a stone and say, "The mountain is a million times the size of this." You will have to see an actual mountain, at least from a distance.

Take as much bliss as you can from Me and leave Me with all your sorrows. My only desire is your happiness. Your happiness is my happiness. I have no happiness apart from yours.

My affection and love for you is that of a thousand mothers.

The calamity that has befallen mankind will be averted. A new Golden Age will occur. I shall not fail. It is not in the nature of Avatars to fail! Avatars insist on Righteousness (Right Action). I always speak of Righteousness, for I have come to re-establish it. I have no other work here.

Realising God within you as the Motivator is the task for which God comes in Human Form.

# Chapter Two

# SAI BABA'S
# SPIRITUAL TEACHINGS

Sai Baba says 'His life is His message'. He has come to teach us that our spirit/soul part of us is really a part of God, which is installed in our hearts. We are <u>not</u> the body or the mind, we are separate from this. Our spirit/soul is our <u>true reality</u>. Sai Baba refers to the spirit/soul as the Atma. Baba says I alone am present in each one of you. I am not different from you; you are not different from me. I am you and you are me. He has come to re-establish the ancient Vedic Teachings and to guide us all on to the spiritual path, the path of love and right action.

Man's soul or human spirit is the indestructible Divine itself. It has come from God, it is part of God. God is the inner reality of all Beings. The human body is a Gift from God to each one of you.

Humanity is the embodiment of divine bliss, wisdom absolute, beyond the pair of opposites, expansive and pervasive like the sky, the goal indicated by the aphorism "You are That", one without a second, eternal, pure, unchanging, witness of all functions of the intellect, beyond all mental conditions and the three attributes of purity, restlessness and dullness.

You are the Spirit (Atma) within you. You are the blessed self. My kingdom within you is your Real Home. Change your vision and the world will appear accordingly. Let the eye be charged with the Divine, it will see all as God. It is foolish to try to shape the world. Shape yourself as the embodiment of Peace, Love and Reverence, and then you will see all as Love, Compassion and Humility.

God is the moving force in every person. He is behind all good impulses and all useful attributes. You are all separate beads that are strung together on one thread – GOD.

You may doubt the fact of the omnipresence of God, but if you realise that your body is the Temple of God, your own heart is the Seat of God and that the consciousness in you is simply a Reflection of God, then your meditation room is your body itself and so God is present wherever you go.

Every religion looks for God and they look far and wide, but man should know that God is omnipresent and resides in the very heart of man.

The Vedas have not emanated from any human individual. They are, in fact,

words and sounds that have been uttered by God: The sacred Vedas spell out the nature of Righteousness. The Vedas give the key to Wisdom. They are God's Laws – the Universal Laws.

The Vedas are God's breath. They declare that God is the inner reality of <u>all</u> <u>beings</u>. All is enveloped by God. All is God. The fundamental lesson that the Vedas seek to install is that there is only **one** not two. The Vedas proclaim that God is one, that the goal is the same and that truth stands self-revealed when the veil of the world is cast away or torn off.

Welcome all religions as kith and kin. The Vedas are the great-grandfather. Buddhism is the son. Christianity is the grandson.

The body is a house, given to you for rent; the owner is God. Live there as long as He wills, thanking Him and paying Him rent with faith and devotion.

There are millions of living beings in this world. All of them have originated from God. Therefore, the same God is present in all of them. People give many names to God, such as Rama, Allah, Jesus, etc. but God is only <u>One</u>. Atma is another name of God; it is the same in everyone. The real name of Atma is Love. Love is only one, but it is present everywhere and can alleviate all sufferings. One who is endowed with love is free from all sufferings.

You may say that progress is possible only through My Grace, but though my heart is as soft as butter, it melts only where there is some warmth in your prayer. Unless you make some disciplined effort, Grace cannot descend on you. The yearning, the agony, of unfulfilled aim, that is the warmth that melts my heart. That is the anguish that wins grace.

Where is God? When we ask ourselves earnestly "Where is God?" We get an instantaneous response from within. You must realise that the Divine is present in everything. Only when you can recognize the Omnipresence of the Divine will you be able to experience the Divine.

The body is the temple of the individual soul; the world is the temple of the universal soul. Use all your talents for serving others; that is the best way of serving yourself, for they and you are one entity.

The fulfillment of human life consists in the service man renders in a spirit of selflessness. A body that is not used to serve others is nothing but a corpse. Hands that help are holier than lips that pray.

I do not want your devotion, I want your transformation. Time waste is life waste.

The treasure that is precious is the quality of even-mindedness in all situations.

Believe firmly that the body is the residence of God and that the food you eat is the offering you make to your deity; that bathing of the divine spirit within you; that the ground you walk upon is His domain; that the joy you derive is His gift; that the grief you experience is His lesson that you may tread the path more carefully.

Forms may vary, but the indwelling spirit is one and the same in all. Hence you should bear no ill-will towards anyone.

Do not do unto another which you would not like to be done unto yourself. For the other is really 'you'.

Your true fame does not depend on your physical beauty or your charm. It does not depend on your riches. It does not depend on your physical strength. It depends only on your Good Character.

Love removes all egoism. Love is selflessness, self is lovelessness. Love, not lust, is the essence of a happy life.

Make the body obey your will. Never give in to it and follow its whims. Be prepared to put it aside. Resolve to keep it under strict control. You have to deal with your body carefully and train it with strict attention. You will develop virtues and the body will become suitable for meditation and spiritual disciplines.

Practise silence, for the voice of God can be heard in the region of the heart only when the tongue is still. It is only in the depths of silence that the voice of God can be heard.

Do not waste time in thoughts such as 'I' and 'mine'. Everything belongs to God.

Be willing to be nothing. Walk this Earth with your head held high, your spirit soaring, your heart opened to love. Believe in yourself and in the GOD within you. Then all will go well.

You need not even read the Scriptures; you will have a divine song especially designed for you if you will but call upon the Lord in your heart.

After long searches here and there, in temples, in churches, on earths and in heavens, at last you come back, completing the circle from where you started, to your own soul, and find that He, for whom you have been seeking all over the world, for whom you have been weeping and praying... on whom you were looking as the mystery of all mysteries shrouded in the clouds is, in reality, the nearest of the near - your own Self (Spirit/Soul).

Through birth and death, through womb and tomb, when the goal is reached, the pilgrim finds that he has travelled from himself to himself.

Sai Baba says "I have come to light the lamp of love in your heart, to see that it shines day by day with added lustre. I have not come to speak on behalf of any religion. I have not come for publicity of any sect or creed or cause, nor have I come to collect followers for any doctrine. I have no plans to attract disciples or devotees to My fold. I have come to tell you of this universal, unitary faith, this path of love, this duty to love, this obligation to love. May you all develop this divine love and stand out as the harbingers of a new age, free from selfishness, greed, hatred and violence. Let each of you be a light to himself or herself, and thereby be a light unto others".

Sai Baba says "For the purpose of your incarnation (your birth) is to grow in love to expand that love, and to merge with God, who is love, and this is best done through service. However many spiritual texts you may read and however many exercises you may do, if you do not allow your heart to melt with compassion, your life will have been a sheer waste. All practices have to be directed towards softening your heart so it will flow with kindness and love.

"Turn to God, drink in the Divine love I offer you and experience the feeling of Divine Bliss which will come when you yourself are so full of love that it overflows and reaches all around you. That is the State of Divine Bliss which leads to Liberation and the Merging with GOD.

"A bubble is on water, from water and merges in water. Man is born in God and merges in God.

"Those who seek the bliss of the supreme should not always run after the joys of sense objects. Live moderately, be comfortable without being lavish.

"The only wealth you carry with you after death is the love of the Lord. You should strive to earn that love during your life. This can be done only by selfless love and by devotion. To earn God's love, you have to dedicate your time, your body and your action to the service of the Lord".

Humility is the sign of an advanced soul. When you witness true humility you will see true love flowing, for the one complements the other.

For devotion to God only two things are needed; Faith and Experience. Both of these are rooted in love.

The purpose of your incarnation (your birth) is to grow in love, to expand that love, and to merge with God who is love, and this is best done through service. Of what good is it to worship the Lord and to ignore Man, his counterpart on Earth? Love for God must be manifested as love for Man.

Silence is the speech of the spiritual seeker. Soft, sweet speech is the expression of genuine love. Hate screeches, fear squeals, conceit trumpets, but love alone sings lullabies.

The Grace of God cannot be won through the gymnastics of reason, the contortions of yoga or the denials of asceticism. Love alone can win it. The Love that knows no bargaining, the Love that is paid gladly as a tribute to the All Loving.

It is enough to cultivate the love that knows no distinction between oneself and another – because all are limbs of the one body of Almighty God.

LOVE - will awaken the compassion in Man towards all God's children. It will make him blind to the failings and faults of others, and aware of his own. It will fill him with wonder and amazement at the handiwork of God, and will enable him to see Divinity everywhere and in everything.

The quickest and most direct way to God is to fill the day with love. God is Love - Love is God. The cultivation of love is the greatest need today. This love alone can save the world. If you develop love, you do not need to develop anything else.

You need to offer only two things to God: pure love and selfless service. Develop truth and love and you need not even pray to Me for everything will be added to you unasked.

Eyes that radiate love will always be twinkling and happy. The person who is steeped in love is always in equanimity.

Service is the utilization of time and skill to the upliftment of society that is the highest form of adoration which God will reward with grace.

When you offer milk to a hungry child or a blanket to a shivering brother on the pavement, you are but placing a gift of God into the hands of another gift of God! God serves, but He allows you to claim that you have served. Try as far as possible within your means to satisfy the needs of the poor, who are God's poor. Share with them whatever food you have and make them happy, at least that once.

Man justifies himself, and proves his claim to be a worthy individual, only through service undertaken sincerely, selflessly and with no thought of worldly reward. It is through service that man can redeem his life.

Service is the only path to self-realisation. It is the highest expression of love. You have to expand yourself in service until the very last breath.

The ideal of a high material standard of living has played havoc with society. We need morality, humility, detachment and compassion, so that the greed for luxury and conspicuous consumption is destroyed.

Who is the richest man? One who has the largest wants – and therefore the largest troubles and worries – or one who is satisfied just with the barest necessities of life and is, therefore, more or less desire-less and so is comparatively happy? Judged by this criterion of happiness, the poor are spiritually rich, while the rich are spiritually poor.

Abstain from the tenfold errors: Injury to life; Adulterous desire; Theft; Misleading statements; Cruel Speech; Jealous talk; The telling of lies; Greed; Envy; The denial of the reality of God.

Be very careful about your speech. Animals have horns, insects have stings, beasts have claws and fangs, but man's biggest weapon of offence is his tongue. The wounds that the tongue inflicts can scarce be healed; they fester in the heart for a very long time.

To speak ill of others is to speak ill of the Divine. If we do not like a certain individual, leave him to himself, be indifferent to him. Why single him out for censure and speak ill of him? You do not know yourself, so how can you know what others are like?

Instead of searching for the faults of others, examine yourself for personal faults that need to be corrected. It is far better to root out your personal faults, if you have any, than to discover hundreds of faults in others.

Do not do anything to bring tears to the eyes of your parents. Honour them and obey them. Do not condemn them as being 'Old Fashioned', old is Gold.

Drop these stupid habits and attachments, wake up and see how hollow is the life that some of you are leading, for life without Love and life without God is totally empty and unfulfilling. Make the decision today to DO something about it.

Nothing is cast away by the mind. As a consequence grief, anxiety and misery continue to simmer in it. The mind can be taught renunciation and one can become a spiritually serene person.

## WATCH

W - Watch your Words

A - Watch your Actions

T - Watch your Thoughts

C - Watch your Character

H - Watch your Heart.

Right at the outset of your spiritual journey you have to make determined efforts to control your desires and anger, your attachments and hatred. This will permit the Divine principle to shine forth from within you. Controlling desire and anger is a most important spiritual practice. It is the primary task of every devotee. If you succeed in controlling desire and anger, attachment and hatred, you will be able to justify your life and reach your goal. But if you allow them to remain within you, then whatever spiritual exercises you undertake will be wasted and your life too will become an utter waste.

Reading is not enough. You might master all the Commentaries and be able to argue and discuss these texts with great scholars, but without attempting to practise what they teach, reading is a waste of time.

Take failure, if it comes, as a challenge to further effort.

Analyze the reasons for your failure and profit by that experience. Learn, as students of Truth how to succeed in the turmoil of life and how to live without causing pain to others and without suffering pain yourself.

When you succeed, ascribe the success to the Grace of God, who urged you on. When you fail, however, ascribe the failure to your own inadequacy.

Put Me (God) first in everything, then all shall be added unto you. Be at peace. Striving gets you nowhere. It simply leaves you exhausted and frustrated because you never seem to be nearer the goal. Just learn to *be*. When you have ceased striving, crawl into My loving arms.

If you are swayed by the possessive attitude, thinking only of yourself, your people, your things, you can be certain that sooner or later you will be cast into sorrow. You must shift your focus away from your 'little self' and its concerns for 'me' and 'mine'. Align yourself with the Will of the Divine. In particular, you should never allow selfishness, pride and jealousy to take up residence within you. These three are the worst of the bad traits that infest man.

True detachment means realising the temporary nature of objects and not allowing your mind to get attached to these transient (impermanent) things. It does not necessarily mean that you feel disgust or hatred for them; it means that you feel no mental attachment towards them. Totally giving up all the objects of the phenomenal world is not possible. However, you can give up your my-ness, your sense of possessiveness. Once you give that up, then you can go ahead and enjoy the various objects of the world. They will cause you no harm.

Life without desire brings divinity to man. Those who see My grace must shed desire and greed. Riches provide a fatal temptation. They are the source and cause of human bondage. The desire to raise the standard of life can never be satisfied.

Tolerate all kinds of persons and various opinions, all attitudes and peculiarities. The school, the home and society are all training grounds for tolerance.

You must surrender your judgement to the Lord and then the Lord will assume full responsibility and will be your Guardian, your Guide and your Motive Power.

Worship God with purity of feeling and free from all other thoughts. As a result of this worship, the Lord will appear before your inner eye, in the form which is dear to you. This vision is not a matter of imagination; it is a 'face to face' experience.

Life is just a play and the Lord has assigned you a part. Act well your part; there all your duty ends. He has designed the play and He enjoys it.

The time will come when the whole of this dream will vanish. To every one of us, there must come a time when the whole universe will be found to have been a dream, when we find that the soul is infinitely better than the surroundings. It is only a question of time, and time is nothing in the infinite.

A boat is meant to go into the water, but the water must not get into the boat. In the same way, we are meant to live in the world, but the world must not get into us.

There is only one Religion - the Religion of Love.

There is only one Caste - the Caste of Humanity.

There is only one Language - the Language of the Heart.

There is only one God, and He is Omnipresent.

Truly there is only one religion – the religion of Love. But on earth there are

many religions, all of which lead along the same path to the ultimate omnipresent God. Call God by any name, because all names belong to God.

Hold fast to the God you believe in, despite the trials and tests, the ups and downs of life. Win the grace of your own subconscious, so that it may accept the Grace of God which is ever available. God does not deny anyone; it is only you who deny God.

Indian philosophy has been classified according to those who believe in God and those who do not believe in God. But to the Divinity, what counts are the 'qualities of men's characters' rather than their beliefs.

There are two duties to be performed by Man: one is to work for the good of the world; the other is work for the liberation of consciousness. The former will drop away once you have become spiritually ready.

If you do good, you receive good from those around you and from the universal entity, God. If you do bad, you receive bad. Divinity only Resounds, Reflects, Re-acts; God has no favourites, no prejudices.

Reduce the luggage that you carry about when on the journey of life. Remember that all that is not 'you' is luggage. The mind, the senses, the intelligence, the imagination, the desires, the prejudices, the discontent, the stress – all these are items of luggage. Jettison them soon, to make your travel lighter, safer and more comfortable.

Running after external things produces all this discontent. That type of desire has no end. It is an unquenchable thirst. But I call you to me and even grant worldly boons so that you may turn Godward.

So long as there is a trace of ego you cannot see the world clearly. Egoism will be destroyed if you constantly tell yourself: "It is He not I. He is the force, I am but the instrument".

For faults and sins committed in ignorance, repent sincerely; try not to repeat the faults and sins. Pray to God to bless you with the strength and the courage needed to stick to the right path.

If your faults are pointed out to you, do not develop a grudge. Carefully examine your own conduct and thankfully proceed to correct yourself.

Once you take on the name of the Lord, which is sweetness itself, it will awaken all the sweetness latent in you. Once you have tasted that joy, you can never for a moment exist without its sustenance. It becomes as essential as air for the lungs.

The main cause of the highest bliss is dedication to God; nothing else can give that genuine and lasting joy.

Why worry when God, in order to make a lovely jewel of you, heats and melts, cuts and carves and removes, your dross in the crucible of suffering?

Turn the key in the lock to the right, it opens; turn the same key to the left, it is locked. So, too, turn your mind to the objective world, it is locked, caught, entangled. Turn it away from the objects of the senses, the lock is loosened and you are Free.

Do not demean yourself as weak, sinful, conceited and wicked. When you demean yourself and condemn yourself, remember you are demeaning and condemning God, who is your Inner Self.

God is the Inner Reality of All Beings. The human body is a Gift from God to each one of you. I have come to light the lamp of love in your hearts.

God is omnipresent (everywhere). Be always and everywhere conscious of the

presence of God. Be vigilant, even while engaged in little tasks. Maintain silence in the recesses of your heart as well as outside.

No one can train another person in meditation. It is possible to teach pose, posture and breathing, but meditation is a function of the inner man. It involves deep subjective quiet, the emptying of the mind and the filling of oneself with the light that emerges from the divine spark within. No textbook or teacher can teach this.

To rise above pain one should meditate and chant God's name. Without meditation, it is not possible to control and master the mind. Thus, meditation is essential to immerse the mind in Supreme Consciousness.

Man extols God as omnipresent, omniscient and omnipotent – but he ignores His presence in himself! God is in the heart of every human being. All of humanity are cells in the Divine Organism.

Give up attachment to worldly possessions. Work hard, do your duty, overcome the five senses. Be loving, begin to perceive your Conscience (Inner Voice) and follow it. Meditate and find God, who resides above, below, around and within you.

Try to avoid killing, adultery, theft, drinking intoxicants and the eating of the flesh. It is of great help in living the highest life if these are kept as far away from as possible.

However busy a man is, observe him – he does not miss his breakfast, lunch or dinner! In like manner, one should take care of spiritual sustenance. They should be fixed times for both prayer and meditation.

There are four things in which every man must interest himself: who am I? from where have I come? Whither am I going? How long shall I be there?

All the chaos in the world is due to the fact that people lead double lives. They say one thing and do another. There should be unity in thought, word and deed.

When troubles come, look beyond the mountains to the blue skies. See that you are only witnessing My Play. See that this life is as temporary as the dancing clouds. Your coming and going is just a part of the performance... The whole world is illusion, all attachments are illusion, family life is illusion, death is illusion, all that you see and think is illusion. This life itself is an illusion!

But never forget that the world is made up only of the five elements. It has no eternal value. Your body also consists only of the five elements. As long as you consider this world real, you will tend to have attachments to the body and to a given place. It is best if you do not waste your time caught up with these attachments. Instead, always remember the goal.

Life is a game - play it

Life is a challenge - meet it

Life is a dream - realise it

Life is love - enjoy it!

The whole world is today in the throes of anxiety and fear. But I can assure you that very soon the dark clouds will be scattered and you will witness a happy era all over the world. Right will be restored and evil will be put down.

Your duty is to yearn for the attainment of the consciousness of the ONE behind all this apparent multiplicity. Be centres of love, compassion, service and mutual Tolerance and – be happy, very, very happy!

Do not get lost in the world aspiring for impermanent joys, impermanent wealth, impermanent position and luxuries. There is no objection to your enjoying the happiness which comes your way.

Take up the name of God any of the innumerable ones, the one that appeals to you most, and the form appropriate to that name and start repeating it from now on: that is the royal road to ensure joy and peace.

Remember, that which is holier than all holy objects is the

name of GOD, which can transform the lower nature and purify it into nectar.

When you tell the truth, tell it clearly and sweetly. Do not tell the truth in an unclear way or tell the untruth in a dear way.

The nearer and dearer you are to Me the greater are your chances of getting burned. You are like a cake: I stir, I knead, I pound, I twist, and I bake. I have come to reform you, to transmute you.

Open your heart to pain, as you would to pleasure for it is My Will, wrought by Me for your good. Welcome it as a challenge. Turn within and derive strength to bear it and to benefit by it.

I am happiest when a person carrying a heavy load of misery comes to Me, for he is the most in need of what I have to give.

Assume silence when you are invaded by anger or remember the name of God. Do not try to remind yourself of things which will inflame your mind and feelings even more.

Control of speech is most important. Excessive talk should be avoided. Speech should be sweet and well intentioned.

People aspire only for the fruits of authority. They shirk the responsibilities that authority involves. Power is sought, but the burden that comes with power is not welcomed. The chaos and the misery in the world today are the creation of those persons who have climbed to positions of authority but do not discharge their responsibilities.

Be careful of the success you have won in the cultivation of virtue and beneficial habits. Often what has been gained is frittered away by keeping trite company, by being critical or lazy, or by talking loosely.

A bullock that does not yield to the yoke; a horse that resists the reins; a car without brakes, a person who knows no self-control; all are equally heading towards disaster!

Do not blame others by pointing out their faults. You will find, upon self-examination, that the faults that you see in others are in you. When you correct yourself, the world becomes correct.

Do not condemn yourselves as sinners; sin is a misnomer for what are really errors. I shall pardon all your errors, provided you repent sincerely and resolve not to follow evil again. Pray to the Lord to give you strength to overcome the habits that enticed you when you were ignorant.

Depending upon the thought you have, you will come to regard the object of your thoughts accordingly. If you are motivated by a sense of love, everything around you takes the form of love. If you have hatred in your heart, you will look upon everything with hatred.

Do not condemn the mind as a monkey etc. It is a fine instrument, with which you can win either liberation or bondage. It all depends on how you manipulate it. It will carry out your orders to the smallest detail. It will lead you, if you so desire, along the royal road right up to the door of Realisation. Or it will make you wander about in the blind alleys, where every step lands you in dirt.

The ego is most easily destroyed by devotion to God, by dwelling on the magnificence of the Lord and through humility and service to others as the children of the Lord.

The greatest instrument by which spiritual success can be measured is true love of God. That will give health, wealth and prosperity.

People suffer because they have all kinds of unreasonable desires and they yearn to fulfil them, but fail. If you look upon Nature and all created objects with the insight derived from inner vision, then attachments will slide away. Attachments to Nature have limits but attachment to God, which you develop when the inner eye opens, has no limits.

Only the man who gives up his own self-interest, regards the happiness of others as his own happiness and devotes himself to their well-being is a truly selfless person.

Take failure, if it comes, as a challenge to further effort. Analyze the reasons for your failure and profit by that experience. Learn, as students of truth, how to succeed in the turmoil of life and how to live without causing pain to others and without suffering pain yourself.

All the time and energy spent in reading the Scriptures is sheer waste, if study and reflection do not help you to recognize that an underlined mind is the real enemy.

Brightness in the face, splendour in the eye, a determined look, a noble gaze, a pleasant voice, open-hearted charity, unwavering goodness: these are signs of a progressing will to attain the vision of God.

God will grant you what you need and deserve; there is no need to ask, no reason to grumble. Be content; be grateful, for whatever happens, whenever it happens. Nothing can happen against His will.

Just as a person with no breath in him becomes useless, similarly, life without truth is useless and becomes a dwelling place of strife and grief.

Simply giving up external activities connected with the satisfaction of sensory desires is not enough; the internal craving has to be uprooted.

Man cannot exist without God sustaining him. God too needs Man in order to announce Himself.

Do not listen to what others say; believe in your own experience. Whatever gives you peace and joy, believe in that. That is the real basis of faith.

You must not be a bit of blotting paper, absorbing all the passions and emotions, all the joys and grief that the actress Nature demonstrates on the sea of life. You must be as a lotus, unfolding its petals when the sun rises in the sky, unaffected either by the slush where it is born or by the water which sustains it.

Man must have equal sight. He must look upon all beings with as much love and faith as he has for himself. For there is nothing evil in creation. Evil appears only as such through faulty vision. Creation gets coloured by the nature of the glasses Man wears. By itself it is eternally pure and holy.

Pride is one of the worst enemies of the spiritual life. If you are conceited, then you are a devotee of the wrong thing.

Come to me, eager to learn, to progress, to see yourself in me, and I shall certainly welcome you and show you the way. You will indeed be blessed.

Merely finishing the study of book after book serves no purpose, but the practice of one line from any one book is enough to save you from aeons of darkness, of ignorance and of yearning for light.

God is the ocean, you are the waves – realise this and be FREE!

Take refuge in the almighty God who resides in your heart, feel that you are always in His hands and therefore always safe.

Where there is righteousness in the heart, there will be beauty in the character. If there is beauty in the character, there will be harmony in the home. Where there is harmony in the home, there will be order in the nation. When there is order in the nation, there will be peace in the world.

The day when we understand that everything belongs to God; that day will be the dawning of KNOWLEDGE.

# SAI BABA'S SPIRITUAL TEACHINGS

## (taken from the Sanathana Sarathi magazines from November 2004 to December 2005)

God is the source and sustenance of all creation. No one can question why God acts in a particular manner. He is the Supreme Lord of the universe and He can act according to His Will. The creation, sustenance and dissolution of the universe are all His Will. But whatever He does is only for the good of the world. Every act in this world, even the tiniest one, is happening as per the Will of God.

Many people in this world are not able to know the reality due to their delusion. God is the only reality. He is your mother, father and friend. Develop firm conviction that He is everything for you. Then God will always take care of you. When you cultivate feelings of oneness, all divine qualities will become manifest in you. You will be an ideal to the world. Then, you will be free from suffering, pain and death. You will realise your true identity.

There are countless people in this world with various types of qualities. Also, there are many people who strive hard to develop their intelligence. But there are very few who strive to cultivate noble qualities. Without cultivating noble qualities, what is the use of intelligence alone? All ancient Rishis (holy men) exhorted people to cultivate noble qualities. It is a great mistake to consider oneself very intelligent and well educated merely because one has acquired high degrees. Mere intelligence and acquisition of high degrees in education are of little use. One has to cultivate noble qualities along with education and intelligence. Intelligence without noble qualities is useless.

Though man is able to occupy high positions in worldly life with his intelligence, it is of no use without noble qualities. Today man is losing faith in God. Faith is like the eyes of man. Devoid of faith, man is blind. Only when he has faith in God can he have faith in everybody else. Therefore, the need of the hour is that man should deepen his faith. With faith in God one can achieve success in all one's endeavours. One who has faith in God will be able to develop faith in everybody. The world is permeated by God and God is the indweller of all beings.

People today have forgotten God and are craving for fleeting pleasures. Nothing is permanent in this world. All your worldly relations are temporary. Your life itself is temporary. Such being the case, how can you consider someone as your permanent friend? There is only one permanent friend; He is God. If you want to experience true love, have full faith in God. God's love is steady. It never diminishes. You are His and He is yours. There is no third person between you and God. God is your only true friend.

Man today believes everything in this world, even that which he has not seen. But he is not prepared to believe that which is right in front of his eyes, the manifestation of divinity in so many ways.

Never forget love. Love is the form of God. Love is God. Live in love. Only then can you understand the reality. Do not go by what others say. Never lose faith in God under any circumstances. Sometimes, even your parents may try to dissuade you from taking the Godward path. You should tell them that God means everything to you; He is your true friend.

You may forget God, but He will never forget you. He will be with you even after your death. Hence, treat God as your true friend. Ultimately, you will become one with Him.

Never be under the mistaken notion that God is outside. God is not outside; God is inside (installed in your heart). God is always in you. Your reflection is God's reflection. Your reaction and resound are His reaction and resound. Everything is basically divine. It is God who makes you play your role in this cosmic drama. It is He who makes you sing, dance etc. He is the cosmic play director. You may call Him by any name. Names may be different but God is one.

If you want to attain God, develop a feeling of oneness with total faith. Then, you will certainly be able to see and experience Him.

I have not come to collect disciples for any particular sect, creed or religion, such as the Hindu religion. I have come to light the lamp of love in the hearts of all humanity.

Utilize every small opportunity to serve your country and society. Even a little help given to an old woman who you come across on the way is service. Do not ever think "What do I gain by helping this woman?" There is great merit even in such a small service. Therefore, continue to serve. There is no greater spiritual exercise than service to fellow human beings. You should not mind any inconvenience that you may undergo while serving others.

People today are not aware where they have come from and where they are going. Only after going through such experiences do they develop firm faith. Without realising the value of human birth, they spend their time in eating and drinking. However, it should be understood that man has taken birth in this world not merely for enjoying food and drink. The be-all and end-all of human life is not merely food, drink, sleep and death. There are higher goals in life that one has to achieve. The purpose of human birth is not merely to enjoy food and comforts. It is not even to acquire education either. The purpose of human birth is totally different, though people have forgotten it. You have to fulfill the real purpose of your birth. The body comes, grows and dies. Before the body dies, one has to fulfill the real purpose for which one has come into this world. One should redeem one's life by engaging oneself in the service of others.

You are not the body. The body is only an instrument and a

means for achieving something higher and noble. It has to be put to use for achieving these higher and more noble aims. The body is like the dress we wear. One day or the other, the body is bound to decay. Till then it has to be maintained properly.

Having been born as human beings, we must dedicate our lives in the service of God and in the constant contemplation of God. If you do so, none of the physical ailments will trouble you. You should get rid of body attachment and develop spiritual consciousness.

The body is bound to suffer. Body is like a water bubble. Mind is like a mad monkey. Don't follow the body; don't follow the mind; follow the conscience.

The body has been given to you for performing sacred actions. The body is a gift from God. For what purpose has God given us this body? It is only for dedicating it in the service of God by helping others. You should always be prepared to dedicate your life to serve society.

Love must be manifested as Service. Service must take the form of food for the hungry, solace for the forlorn, consolation for the sick and the suffering. Jesus wore himself out in such Service. The heart full of compassion is the temple of God. Compassion was his message. Jesus was sorely distressed at the sight of the poor. Today Jesus is worshipped but his teachings are neglected. Develop compassion. Live in love. Be good, do good and see good. This is the way to God.

Today man is losing faith in God. Therefore, the need of the hour is that man should deepen his faith. With faith in God one can achieve success in all one's endeavours. One who has faith in God will be able to develop faith in everybody. Only such a person can realise that God is immanent in every living being. The world is permeated by God and <u>God is the indweller of all beings</u>.

The purpose of human birth is not to spend life aimlessly and finally depart from this world, only to be born again and again from the womb of the mother. There is a specific purpose for which one is born in this world. Therefore one has to realise that purpose and sanctify one's life. Our education, our work and the money we earn, all these must be spent in a purposeful way.

You do not know why you are here in this world, what you have to know, where you have to go and, by knowing, what you can reach there. Being ignorant of all this, your entire life is wasted. Therefore, you should make efforts to understand why you have come here, what your reality is and where you have to go.

Do not pray to God for the fulfillment of your worldly desires. Instead, leave everything to God's Will. Have full faith that He will do what is good for you. Pray to Him: "Oh God, please take care of us every moment of our life."

God pervades the entire world in the form of the five elements, namely, space, wind, fire, water and earth. In mankind, these elements connote the faculties of hearing, touch, sight, taste and smell respectively. There isn't a place where these five elements are not present. God permeates the entire universe. That is why it is said that all hands, feet, eyes, heads, mouths and ears are His. The elders in the past therefore declared that God is present everywhere; there is no place where God is not present.

How can we comprehend the principle of this all-pervasive divinity? People attribute various names and forms to God. They celebrate the birthdays of their chosen deities, worship them and derive joy from doing this. But it is not possible for anyone to fathom fully the nature of divinity. It is not possible to attribute any form to God. He is beyond all names, forms and attributes. God has neither birth nor death. How can anyone give a specific name to God, who is all-powerful and all-pervasive?

Whatever God does is for the welfare of the world. You must understand that world is the very form of God. The Creator and creation are not different from each other. We should not worship God for the fulfillment of worldly desires. We should pray to God to attain Him. He showers His grace on all. It is God who gives us everything. He alone knows what is good for us. Everything that we need is provided by Him. However, it is not the quality of a true devotee to feel disappointed and blame God if his desires are not fulfilled. It is our duty to find ways and means to earn God's grace and make efforts to attain Him. Nobody can understand or explain divine plans. God alone knows His plans and only He can reveal them. No one can comprehend the ways of God.

Food and water are the gifts of God. Mankind cannot create food and water by himself. He does not even know what type of food is essential to lead a healthy life. He should, in fact, make efforts to understand this.

Any mighty task can be accomplished by prayer. Hence, pray to God silently. Do not pray for the fulfillment of your petty desires. Give up all desires and pray to God wholeheartedly with love. You will certainly find fulfillment in life. You can understand and experience divinity only through love. Nothing can be achieved without love. Love makes all your tasks successful.

Love is the essence of My teachings. My power is the power of love. There is nothing greater than love. When you develop love, you can easily face the challenges of life and emerge victorious. God will always be with you, in you and around you and will take care of you. However, your prayer should be sincere. Say what is there in your mind. Baba (God) is within you; He knows your thoughts and feelings. Develop unity of thought, word and deed.

No one can predict when God will shower His grace on an individual. Only God knows the answers to questions like who, when, where, why and how. If one forgets God and gets carried away by ego, one will not meet with success in one's endeavours. Anything can be achieved through prayer. There is nothing greater than prayer. Hence, everyone must necessarily offer his prayer to God. However, one should not pray for worldly gains. "Oh God! I want your love and nothing else" - this should be your constant prayer. Once you become the recipient of God's love, you can conquer the entire world. If your prayers are sincere, they will certainly be answered. There is nothing that God cannot accomplish. God's Will takes shape at the appropriate time without any prompting or planning.

Jesus was the son of God. While he was being crucified, he said, "Oh Father, Let Thy Will be done." When you surrender yourself to God's Will, He will take care of you.

Do not develop pride. Give up ego and ostentation. Pray silently and sincerely. Then your prayers will surely be answered. God is not confined to a place somewhere in a distant corner. He always resides in your heart. He can accomplish anything. He is ever ready to perform any task, big or small, for His devotees. All are His children. Hence, He will certainly answer your prayers. Jesus taught: "All are the children of God." When you have such firm conviction, you can accomplish any task. You need not read voluminous books. Fill your heart with love and leave everything to His Will.

It is only love that will help you to achieve success in your life. Hence, develop love. That is the true prayer God expects from you.

There is no other path except that of love to attain God. Love is God, God is love. But people do not understand what love is. They consider attachment to all that is worldly and material as love. Out of their selfishness, they love worldly objects and materials. So, man's love today is tainted with selfishness. There is selfish motive behind whatever he does. How then can man have the vision of God, who is the very embodiment of selfless love? Love is present in all beings, right from the ignorant person to the realised person. How can one describe such a principle of love?

Ego and pomp have become rampant today. Desires have become limitless. Man's heart is filled with selfishness and compassion has no place in it. That is the reason why he is unable to have the vision of the Divine Spirit and experience bliss. I always speak about the principle of love. I do not know anything other than love. When divinity is uniformly present in all, how can you share your love with some and deny it to others? How can anyone say, "Love this and not that"? God has no specific form. But if you firmly resolve to see God and make sincere efforts, God will assume a form and manifest before you.

There is love in every one of you. Love is not limited to human beings alone but is present in all living beings. Every being is endowed with the quality of supreme divine love. One has to give up enmity and cultivate unity and purity in order to understand this truth.

Love cannot be explained in words. It can only be experienced and enjoyed. The experience of love confers bliss on us. Hence, we can say that bliss is the form of love.

Everything in this world is bound to change except the principle of love. Love is the only true and eternal path which will lead you to divinity. Divinity is present in all in the form of love, but each one experiences it in his own way.

One whose heart is filled with love will see the manifestation of divinity everywhere. It is a mistake to think that Nature is different from God. People give various names to divinity based on their own experience. Jewels are many, but gold is one. Likewise, names and forms are different, but divinity is one.

Consider everyone as divine. The Cosmic Being has thousands of heads, eyes and feet. All heads, all eyes and all feet are His. Such transcendental divinity can be experienced only in absolute silence and in solitude. There lies hidden sacred divine power in the depth of total silence. The tongue is given to you not to indulge in vain gossip. That is why the ancient sages and seers practised silence. It is possible to experience God only in the depth of silence.

However, we should understand the true meaning of silence. Silence does not mean merely refraining from speech. It is much higher that that and includes the mind also. The transcendental nature of divinity cannot be described in words. It is beyond the grasp of the mind.

Turn your vision inward and observe absolute silence. Only then can you realise all-pervasive divinity.

God has assumed all the names and forms that we find in the world. Hence, you should develop faith in the existence of God. If you make sincere efforts, you can certainly realise Him.

Today people conduct enquiry and research into various aspects of the world. But divinity cannot be experienced with such enquiry and research. Select a divine form of your choice and contemplate on it. When you focus your mind on the divine form, your mind gets transformed completely and becomes one with divinity.

Whatever you see and experience in the world is only the reaction, reflection and resound of your feelings. Do not get deluded by the reaction, reflection and resound. Turn your mind inward and contemplate the reality within you. You will certainly be able to experience divinity. Divinity is one without a second and is all-pervasive.

Body attachment is the cause of all differences. You will understand and experience unity in diversity only when you give up body attachment. Once you are free from body attachment, you can experience God in a moment. Whatever you see is the manifestation of God. The principle of unity in diversity is divinity. But you are unable to understand and appreciate this truth. In order to understand this truth, there should be total transformation in your feelings.

Hold on to the principle of love firmly and you can achieve anything. When you fill your heart with love, you will be protected wherever you go. Love is the reality and everything else is only <u>reaction</u>, <u>reflection</u> and <u>resound</u>. In order to experience the reality, you have to cultivate steadiness of mind in the first instance. How can you make your mind steady? You have to contemplate on one name and one form. Be firm in your chosen path. Do not get deluded by what appears to the physical eyes. Open the eye of wisdom and see the reality.

Many people ask Me about the proper way of meditation. I always tell only one thing, "Meditation does not mean merely closing your eyes and imagining anything and everything. Choose one form (of God), install it in your heart and see that it is steady.

Have total faith in one name and one form of God and contemplate it. That is true meditation. If you follow this practice earnestly, you can experience divinity.

Make your mind steady and fix it on God. Mind is the cause of everything in this world. Mind by itself does not go anywhere. It is we who direct it and divert it in different ways according to our whims and fancies. We are responsible for its unsteadiness. When you keep your mind steady and focus it on God, you will find the brilliant and blissful form of God wherever you see.

Self-knowledge is that knowledge where everything else becomes known. A person with self-knowledge can indeed be acclaimed as all-knowing. Secular learning cannot confer on us abiding and absolute peace. Self-knowledge alone can help us cross the sea of sorrow. So, all should strive to attain self-knowledge which can be acquired through purity of mind. And purity of mind can be attained through sacred deeds, charity, compassion and devotion.

God does not cause suffering to any living being in His creation. All sorrows and difficulties are of your own making.

God is the protector of all living beings. He provides peace and happiness to one and all. May all the people of the world be happy! This is the Will of God. How then can God cause sorrow to a human being? Unable to understand this truth, you blame God for your suffering.

There is a saying in Telugu (local Indian dialect): "One who is free from worry will be able to sleep peacefully even in a market place." Everyone should make efforts to overcome worries and enjoy everlasting happiness.

Everyone aspires to attain bliss. In fact, that is the very purpose of human life.

Everyone wants to be happy. One should be happy even in difficulties. You need not search for happiness outside. It is always with you, in you, around you. You are unable to experience it, as you have not understood the true meaning of happiness. You are under the illusion that happiness lies in money, wealth and material comforts. Once you have the taste of true happiness, you will not crave worldly possessions. True happiness springs forth from the depth of one's heart. The heart is the source of bliss.

The apparent joy that one experienced is artificial and temporary. Only the happiness that springs from the heart is permanent.

Conduct yourself in a way that does not cause unhappiness to others. You cannot really experience happiness when others are unhappy. Happiness cannot be purchased in a market, nor can it be acquired by worldly means. It should manifest from within.

You should respect others' feelings and act appropriately. You should share your happiness with your fellow men.

You must have observed that small children are always happy and cheerful. They do not have any inhibitions. When somebody smiles at them, they will also smile innocently and make everybody happy. Their happiness is not ordinary happiness that comes and goes. It is that which is inherent in all human beings as their natural quality. It does not come from outside. It is something that comes from within.

True happiness lies in sacrifice and renunciation. Body is the combination of five elements and mind is merely a bundle of thoughts. One should neither be attached to the body nor follow the vagaries of the mind. Drive away the evil qualities of desire, anger, greed, infatuation, pride and jealousy and manifest your inner peace and bliss.

But man today is destroying peace and bliss instead of developing them. He loses his peace even in trivial matters. People say, "I want peace". Where is peace? Is it present outside? If peace were to be found outside, people would have bought it by spending any amount of money. But outside, we find only pieces! The real peace is within.

Whether you boil it hard or dilute it with water, milk remains white. White symbolizes purity. In the same manner, your heart should always remain pure, bright and peaceful in spite of all trials and tribulations. You should subdue sorrow, keep the evil qualities of anger, hatred and jealousy under check and manifest your innate bliss. What is the cause of anger? You become angry when your desires are not fulfilled. So, man can be happy if he keeps his desires under control.

Embodiments of Love! (Sai Baba addresses His devotees in this way).

You are all full of love. In fact, your heart is overflowing with love. There is love in each of you, but you are directing it towards worldly relationships. You have not tasted true love. Love God wholeheartedly. That is true love. People may come and people may go, but God neither comes nor goes. He is always present. When you are engulfed in sorrow, think of happiness. Then and there, you will experience happiness.

Bliss is very much immanent in every human being. Wherever we are, whatever be the position we occupy, our essential nature is bliss.

Body is like a water bubble; mind is like a mad monkey. Don't follow the mind; don't follow the body. After all, why should one feel sorry about the body and mind, which are transient? In fact, bliss is our essential nature, which is permanent. Lead your life filled with love. Cultivate love. You can experience bliss when you develop love.

If you can achieve this, you will not be disturbed by sorrows and difficulties. The heart is the seat of bliss. True bliss flows from a pure and loving heart. Try to experience such bliss. All other forms of happiness are momentary.

Happiness is God's gift to man. <u>Happiness is Union with God</u>. You experience real happiness when you unify with God. You cannot experience it when you are separated from Him.

Start the day with love; Fill the day with love; End the day with love; that is the way to God.

Let me remind you once again that neither age nor position, nor for that matter anything in this physical environment, can bring about such bliss. It is only the pure and loving heart that is the source of bliss. Divinity is the only principle that is changeless. God is ever blissful. In fact, He is the embodiment of bliss.

Man makes efforts to experience happiness. You can find no one in the world who does not want to be happy. Happiness is essential for man. But one must understand that happiness cannot be acquired from outside. It comes from the heart. The heart is the source of bliss. The happiness we enjoy in the external world is only a reaction, reflection and resound of the happiness within.

Sadness is of your own making. If you are experiencing sorrow, it is because you have immersed yourself in sorrow. It is possible that you may encounter some ups and downs in life. But they should not mar your blissful nature. See how blissful I am! Not only now, I am always in bliss. In fact, you can also experience this bliss when you come to Me. But if you come with evil thoughts and desires, you cannot experience it. These are your weaknesses. Do away with these weaknesses, which can bring about your ruin.

Do not become a victim of worry. Sorrows and worries are like passing clouds, never give importance to them. Always be happy and peaceful. Peace and happiness are your innate qualities.

Evil ways of man cause natural calamities. The tsunami caused untold misery and suffering to a large number of people. It is only man's evil deeds that are responsible for such a calamity. Therefore, never indulge in wrong actions and evil deeds. It is man who is responsible for the calamity caused by the tsunami, and not God. But man thinks that all such calamities are thrust upon him by God. Never! God always provides happiness to man. He has no anger or hatred. His nature is love.

Strictly speaking, happiness will not have any value without sorrow. Man cannot experience happiness without undergoing some difficulty or another. Both happiness and sorrow are interlinked. One cannot exist without the other.

God's love fills the whole universe and even then it overflows! God's very nature is that of love. Everything has been created through love, every tree, every flower and even every rock. There is only one being where all of this has come from, and that is God.

When you develop correct understanding, you will realise that everything is for your good only. Then you will be immersed in bliss day and night. Treasure this bliss in your heart and share it with one and all. Then you will be all the more blissful.

True spiritual practice is to rise above your sorrows and difficulties. When you constantly think that you are endowed with peace and bliss, no difficulties will bother you.

While taking food, you must always ensure that you eat only that food which you can easily digest. Never consume food which is hard to digest. Just as you feel light and happy before sitting down for eating food, so also you should feel comfortable and light when you get up after eating it. Some people sit for food with a light stomach and get up after overloading it. This is not the proper way of eating. Always eat light food.

You are imprisoned in your ego. Though you should try to liberate yourselves from this bondage quickly and safely, most of you do not seek from Me the key to this liberation.

You ask from Me trash and tinsel, petty little cures and gains. Very few desire to get from Me the thing I have come to give, liberation itself. Even among the few who seek liberation, only a small percentage sincerely stick to the path of spiritual practice and from among them only an infinitesimal number succeed.

There can be no match for the accomplishments of the elders after they cross the age of 60 or 70. Their intellectual acumen and divine qualities can show a new path to mankind. When you realise their great qualities, it will bring about transformation in your own life.

Many people presume that those beyond the age of 70 years are useless and a burden on the family and society. But this is not true. In fact enthusiasm, dynamism and mental strength increase after a person reaches 70. It is only after attaining the age of 70 that man's willpower and spiritual strength develop in full measure. Prior to that, he behaves like an ordinary human being and does not strive to set an example to others. But after the age of 70, man's mental faculties and divine power blossom to the highest extent and prompt him to set new goals in life.

The elders are endowed with exalted and noble thoughts. They set highly valuable ideals for the youngsters. Yet, unable to understand the value of their thoughts, the youngsters disregard them and do not pay any heed to them. It is to be noted with admiration how the elders brought up their children in a proper way with concern and enthusiasm. Unfortunately, today people grudge giving them even one square meal a day. This is highly deplorable.

The world can benefit a lot from elderly people. None can estimate the immense spiritual power they possess. The ancient Rishis (holy men) of India were the embodiments of this great spiritual power. The noble thoughts propounded by them are most valuable. They made marvellous plans for the blissful future of man. The objective behind holding this function is to recognize the great spiritual power of these elders, so that the youngsters are inspired to follow the ideals set by them.

Get rid of demonic qualities and develop humanness. Only then can you rise to the level of divinity. Always remember three things – unity, purity and divinity. Unity implies the oneness of the human race. Where there is unity in humanity, divinity will manifest there.

Everyone should try to realise their innate divinity and enjoy eternal bliss. The divine power latent in a human being has no limits. Whether it is fine arts like music or any other human endeavour, when it is suffused with divine power, it reaches great heights. Offer your talent to God and sanctify your life.

Embodiments of love! Whether one is a pauper or a millionaire, intake of food is natural to every human being. But, having attained the sacred human birth, it is unbecoming of man to spend his entire life merely for the sake of filling his belly. Why don't you spend a few moments in contemplation of God instead of spending your entire lifetime in pursuit of physical comforts? There are, of course, a few people in this land of Bharat (India) who sanctify their time in contemplation of God. But the vast majority of people are wasting their human birth in vain pursuits.

People suffer because they spend all their time and energy in mundane pursuits. They are not able to enjoy mental peace and physical comforts in full measure. The body is like a water bubble. It is nothing but a bundle of bones. Mind is like a mad monkey. It is a mistake to strive for the pleasure of the transient body and wavering mind. It is, of course, the duty of every human being to make efforts to keep the body healthy, so that he is not dependent on others. But many people spend their entire life in pursuit of physical comforts and pleasures. There are only a few who are centred on eternal peace and happiness.

Do not be under the mistaken impression that the body is meant for eating and enjoying physical pleasures only. Certain duties have been assigned to man which will will enable him to experience happiness at the level of the body, mind, senses and spirit when he performs them. One should enquire what the purpose of human birth is. The goal of man's life is liberation.

The body should be used as an instrument to rise from the level of humanness to divinity. Human life is redeemed only when we experience divinity. There are many people who are making efforts in this direction, but only a few are able to realise the truth and achieve the goal. One may undertake any type of activities, but one should always aspire to attain peace of mind. Without peace of mind, every endeavour of man will only add to his restlessness.

Love is the only wealth that does not diminish. It is the property of God. Therefore, cultivate pure and selfless love. God's love will always follow you wherever you are and will protect you at all times. Do not ever consider that money alone constitutes your wealth. In fact, love is your real wealth. The wealth of love always grows; it never diminishes.

Difficulties come and go. Not only poor people, even a millionaire cannot escape from difficulties. Do not be depressed or bogged down by small problems. The physical body may undergo difficulties but you should see to it that your mind rests in peace. Mind is the basis of happiness for everyone. All physical comforts will be of little use without peace of mind. Only through contemplation of God can you attain peace of mind and not by any other means.

Even when you are undergoing difficulties, always think that they are meant to bring you happiness. Every human being undergoes difficulties, only to enjoy happiness later.

However, he does not realise this during the period of suffering, but in course of time, when suffering ends and happy days arrive, he would realise the truth. Hence, always remember the truth that sorrows and difficulties are precursors of happy days ahead. In fact, real happiness comes out of difficulties only.

God is the refuge of the poor and the forlorn. He is always with them through all the troubles and worries of life. Do not think that God is in some distant land. God is by your side always. In fact, He is present in the inner recesses of your heart. Never think that God is away from you at any point of time. Neither friends nor relatives can come to your rescue. God is your sole refuge. He will protect you under all circumstances. (He might send a friend or relative to you if you are in trouble, because God uses people as instruments to help others).

In spite of the numerous difficulties, the Bharatiyas (Indians living in India) never swerved from the Godward path.

There are many affluent countries where people lead a luxurious life, but they do not have peace of mind. It is the good fortune of the Bharatiyas that they are able to enjoy peace of mind. Their devotion to God is responsible for this.

You have come here because of your love and devotion to Swami (Sai Baba). Go back to your places with the same feelings of love and devotion. After reaching home, continue to experience the same bliss that you have experienced in the presence of Swami. Then, you will forget all your difficulties and worries. Happiness and sorrow come in our life to develop in us the spirit of equanimity.

Always pray to God before eating your food. By doing so, the food will be sanctified and its essence will be assimilated in your body. Your heart will also be purified.

Do not ascribe any differences or negative feelings to God. You observe negativity in God because of your own negative feelings. God is one; contemplate on Him, worship Him. See divinity and unity everywhere. Never entertain negativity.

Divinity permeates the entire universe. If we analyze carefully it will be obvious that all that we witness around is God' consciousness and nothing else. Wherever we look and whichever form we come across, it is resplendent with God's consciousness, whether it is the form of a child, an elderly person, a woman or a man. How can you describe this all-pervading divine consciousness or limit it to a particular time and place?

People today are creating differences among human beings by attributing different names and forms to nameless, formless and attributeless Gods. This is a serious mistake. Divinity is being divided by devotees. Devotees who divide God are evil-minded. God is one. Never create divisions in the name of God. When we do not realise the oneness of God, we engage ourselves in futile arguments and counter arguments. Whether it is Rama, Krishna, Siva or Vishnu, all these are only different names ascribed by devotees to God. <u>But God is ONE</u>.

People attribute different forms to God and describe Him in many different ways. Each one describes Him according to his imagination, ascribing a particular name and form to Him. But no description can fully reveal Divinity. Nameless, formless God is omnipresent (everywhere) and all-pervading. Neither words can describe nor can the mind comprehend Him. Who can describe such Divinity? Divinity signifies only one thing, that is, consciousness. This consciousness assumes the form that it enters – it may be the form of a dog, a crow, a crane or a human being. Divinity therefore, connotes consciousness. This consciousness is present in all human beings, nay, even in insects, birds, beasts and animals. God assumes all names and forms.

Just as consciousness is the same in all, divine love does not observe any difference between living beings. Your love for your father, mother, brother, sister, etc is based on your earthly relationships with them. But divine love is the same for all. In fact, every living being is the embodiment of divinity. God assumes all names and forms. <u>Hence, you are also the form of God.</u>

Man forgets the Divine because he is deluded by the deep wine of worldliness. God is one and He is present wherever you see, be it a city or a village, sky or deep sea. You can realise God by cultivating love for God. It is only love that binds God. It is this divine love that will help you to understand oneness of God. God is one without a second.

Love for God makes us realise our unity with divinity. When we have fusion with God, there will be no scope for confusion.

Evil company, bad conduct and wrong food habits are responsible for the delusion which makes us see diversity in unity. Once we get rid of them, we will see unity and divinity everywhere. God is present here, there and everywhere.

Today truth and righteousness have declined. However, they cannot be rooted out completely. There is nothing more sacred than truth and righteousness. They ensure peace. It is only the practice of the great human values of Truth, Righteousness, Peace and Love that made India the great spiritual leader of the entire world. Truth and righteousness are essential for peace. Even more essential than anything else today is sacrifice. Sacrifice does not mean giving up all worldly possessions. Real sacrifice lies in putting these human values into practice in our day-to-day life.

It is only God who can save the life of a human being. Some doctors claim that they can give good medicines or perform surgery to save the life of a person. They make several promises, but fail to fulfill them. Apart from God, no one else can save or prolong the life of a person. With God's grace, one can achieve anything in this world. You must strive to earn the grace of God right from your childhood. When you start praying thus from an early age, you will surely earn His grace and protection.

Consider women as embodiments of truth. Even if some minor faults are noticed in them, do not give importance to them. Respect and revere them. Do not use even a single word that would hurt them. If they really wish, they can achieve any great task. You should be prepared to lay down even your life for the sake of protecting and helping women. At least from today, all of you should come forward to protect the honor and dignity of women in the world.

Men should lead a life of truth and righteousness. Only then can they protect the country and become worthy of being called real men. Otherwise, how can they consider themselves worthy of the status of human beings? Several people go to temples. When they visit a temple, they must make a vow that they would respect and protect women.

Only then will they be protected. Only when the women are safe will the whole world be happy.

When you protect Truth and Righteousness, God will, in turn, protect not only you and your country but the whole world. Consider truth as your life-breath and righteousness your armour. If you have these two, you will have everything. You don't need to fight with anybody in the world. The world has not done any harm to you. There is nothing great in attacking those who have done no harm to you.

Only God exists. The world is but an illusion. The sacred teaching of the Vedas should be publicized and should be imparted to everyone. You find many spiritual aspirants chanting and teaching the Vedas. It is fruitless if one does not practise what one preaches. It is like a gramophone record which plays the song but does not experience its melody. So, one should recognize, understand and practise the sacred teachings of the Vedas.

Every thought leaves an impression on the mind, so be ever alert that contact with evil is avoided. Ideas which are opposed to spiritual tendencies, that narrow the limits of love, that provoke anger or cause disgust, have to be shut out. For the aspirant, this is the most essential discipline. One must sublimate such thoughts before they cause an impact on the mind, and concentrate on the very source of the thinking process. This can be achieved by the practice of equanimity, unaffectedness or balance. The path of devotion and dedication is the easiest for most. It is attainable by love, for love leads you quickly to the Goal!

The body is made up of five elements and is bound to perish sooner or later, but the indweller has neither birth nor death. The indweller has no attachment whatsoever and is the eternal witness.

Wherever you look, you cannot find anything more powerful and more valuable than love. There is nothing beyond love. All descriptions to estimate its greatness will be inadequate. In this vast world, there is no human being or living being without love.

It may be easy to give lectures on love, but it is difficult to understand it. Make every effort to comprehend it. If you understand the nature of your love, you will understand the love of others. Love is in you, with you and around you. Once you understand love, you will become the very embodiment of love. If you just talk about love without understanding it, then you cannot become the embodiment of love. The more you understand the principle of love, the nobler you become.

There is no being superior to a human being in intelligence in this world. But human beings are unable to make proper use of their intelligence. They conduct themselves in an unworthy manner because of their selfishness and self-interest. Humans do not lack anything in their life. Everything is at their disposal. But they lack the discrimination to make proper use of the resources available. In spite of having everything in plenty, they are not able to give up their pettiness.

Deep-rooted selfishness and self-interest are making a human being's intelligence perverted and leading them astray. When you give up selfishness, then your power and intelligence will become manifold. Human beings are endowed with immense powers of intelligence, but they are not trying to make proper use of it. Humans are in fact misusing their intelligence due to their ignorance.

Students today read all sorts of books and fill their heads with useless information. There is little use in studying a book if the head is filled with rubbish. Students should acquire the knowledge which will help them to lead a noble life and save them from the cycle of birth and death. They should acquire that knowledge which will make them immortal. Modern students have become proficient in bookish knowledge. They have the intelligence to answer any question from textbooks. But they are not making efforts to translate their bookish knowledge into practical knowledge.

The knowledge one acquires should be utilized for the benefit of society. You should utilize your wealth and knowledge not for selfish purposes, but for the welfare of others. God has given you the human body not merely to eat, sleep and enjoy worldly pleasures. The body is given to you to serve others. Of what use are your education and intelligence if society is not benefited from them? Presently, man is making new discoveries and inventions but to this day he has not really understood the purpose of human birth. It is only by the Grace of God that human beings acquire intelligence, knowledge and wealth. Human beings should understand this and lead a sacred and divine life. They should use their God-given gifts for the welfare of others. But human beings are acting contrary to it and thereby ruining themselves.

Animals like bulls and buffaloes render service to human beings in a number of ways. It is unfortunate that human beings are not able to understand even such a simple thing. Instead of developing humanness, they are acquiring demonic natures, and living a miserable life. One can only attain divinity by serving society.

Despite our high education and intelligence, there is great scope for learning the valuable lessons which Nature teaches us. One can learn even from small creatures like ants, birds and animals. These lessons of life cannot be taught in the classroom. Even teachers are not making efforts to understand the principle of divinity within. Education is not meant merely to eke out a livelihood. You have to share your knowledge with others, give joy to one and all and thereby rise to the level of divinity. Equal-mindedness is the hallmark of a true human being.

Divinity is latent in every human being. But man is becoming weak as he is unable to realise his latent divinity. In order to realise one's divinity, one should cultivate sacred feelings.

I have introduced the 'Educare Program' in the educational institutions. Education is related to worldly knowledge. It can be acquired by going through books, whereas Educare is meant to manifest the latent divinity in man. Education has temporary benefits, whereas Educare bestows everlasting happiness. One cannot become great by mere acquisition of education. One should practise Educare and manifest one's latent qualities.

Educare is the need of the hour. Only through Educare can you realise the divinity which is present in every atom and every cell of your body. In fact, you are seeing divinity every moment, but are unable to recognize this truth. You can call yourself educated only when you recognize divinity which is all-pervasive.

Truly, God has endowed human beings with immense potential. That is love. It is beyond all description and measure. But human beings are frittering away this power without realising its value. They are under the mistaken notion that love means physical and worldly relationships. No, no! This is not true love. True love is that which unites you with one and all. People utter this word repeatedly without actually knowing its meaning. Love does not hurt anybody. It always helps. Hence, consider love as your true property. There is no property more valuable than love in this world.

Humans are misusing the God-given gift of love by diverting it to worldly matters and sensual pleasures. Your foremost duty is to make proper use of love by following the dictum, *Help ever, Hurt never.*

Love is your only true and eternal wealth. But you are misdirecting it towards mean and worldly pursuits. It should be treasured in your heart and utilized for sacred purposes. You may share it with any number of people, it will never diminish. But man today is unable to understand and experience the true spirit of love. Love is the life-breath of every being. In order to understand love, you have to dive deep into the ocean of love.

Love cannot be understood from a superficial level; you have to immerse yourself completely in it. Worldly love is such that you can just taste it and give it up. But divine love is not like that; once you taste it, you will never leave it. Love is God's property. Safeguard and protect this property with utmost care. Love is God, God is love. Hence, you cannot separate love from God. Live in love. That is the only way you can understand love and experience God.

It may be easy to give lectures on love, but it is difficult to understand it. Make every effort to comprehend it. If you understand the nature of your love, you will understand the love of others. Love is in you, with you and around you. Once you understand love, you will become the very embodiment of love. If you just talk about love without understanding it, then you cannot become the embodiment of love. The more you understand the principle of love, the nobler you become. Once you understand the principle of love and put it into practice, others will also try to copy you.

Service is twice blessed. It blesses both, the one who does and the one who receives. Its blessings are twofold. It eradicates ego and confers bliss.

While performing service activities, never consider yourself as the doer. Always think that whatever service activities you are undertaking are for your own upliftment. These service activities must be undertaken to develop self-confidence which will lead to self-satisfaction and self-realisation. Thus, service is meant to realise your true Self. It should never be considered as help for others.

Man has no authority to teach ideals to others without putting them into practice himself first. In fact, he is gifted with human birth to be an ideal in the entire creation. There is immense divine power in human beings. Human beings are not simply 'one with body'. They are endowed with wisdom, constant integrated awareness and discrimination. They should channel these powers in the right direction.

First and foremost, one has to understand the true meaning of *Jnana* (wisdom). Some people think that knowledge acquired by reading numerous books is wisdom. No, this is not correct. Real wisdom is the knowledge that emerges from within oneself. This should be experienced, put into practice and then shared with others. In the ultimate analysis, this would enable one to be greatly benefited and enlightened.

All that we teach to others must be supported by practice. Everything is reaction, reflection and resound of one's own inner being. Every word we utter is the resound of the inner being. Reflection is that which is contemplated upon, experienced and put into practice. Reaction is, however, very important. Reaction comes out of action. Hence our actions must always be pure and sacred. Reaction, reflection and resound occupy an important place in the life of a human being. All the worldly knowledge humans acquire is the product of resound. Resound comes out of reaction and reaction transforms itself into reflection. The unity of these three constitutes humanness.

It may be necessary for you to adapt yourself to modern techniques and new practices from time to time. The world today is undergoing phenomenal changes. All those changes may not be important for you. Nevertheless, you are required to study several branches of knowledge in modern times to cope up with these rapid changes taking place all over the world. However, this study does not constitute 'real knowledge'. Hence, there is no greatness in pursuing secular education. Real knowledge is that which helps you to understand, recognize and realise the principle of the Self. It enables you to recognize your true nature and realise the truth.

Petals have a pattern of their own which lends beauty to the flower. If you sow a seed, it will grow into a plant in the due course of time and yield beautiful flowers. However, the seed by itself is not attractive. When the plant grows and yields flowers, the beauty and fragrance of the flowers will give joy to one and all.

There are several petals in a flower. The flower appears beautiful as long as there are petals in it. Once the petals fade and fall down, the flower ceases to exist. Hence, all of you should form yourself into a beautiful flower. Let everyone experience and enjoy its beauty and fragrance.

It is natural for all living beings to bear the consequences of their actions, good or bad. None can escape from them. Human beings in this world, however, think that they are undergoing suffering without having done anything wrong. But the fact is otherwise. Whatever pleasure or pain one undergoes, it is certainly the outcome of one's actions.

Every human being performs actions and experiences their fruits as a consequence. Nevertheless, he keeps doubting whether it is a natural consequence of his actions or it is due to any unknown reason. Man has been trying to know the truth about this phenomenon, which he experiences in his life without knowing its real cause. Not only human beings but insects, birds and animals have to experience the consequences of their Karmas (actions). For example, bats hang from the branches of a tree with heads downwards. It is their destiny. That is how they are born to live.

It is this inevitable law of Karma which guides the destiny of all living beings; it is the cause of their endless cycle of birth and death. Good Karmas do bear good results and vice versa.

I never complain against anybody, nor do I criticize anyone. True to My name, Sathya, I always adhere to truth. Sathya means Truth.

Bharatiya (Indian) culture enjoins on everyone to believe that the real nature of human beings is supreme and that they should ever be conscious of this truth. The Bharatiyas of past ages had faith in this great reality. They achieved victory in their endeavours as a result of this faith and rose to lofty heights. They reached the peak of progress. We have slid down into the present state mainly because of lost faith in the Atma (Spirit/Soul). Loss of faith in the Atma or Self involves loss of faith in God Himself. That Omnipresence, that inner motivator of all, who is the warp and woof (weft) of our body and mind, our emotions and intellect – strengthening faith in Him is the only means of realising the highest goal of humanity.

Earn God's Grace by serving your parents.

In this world the love of one's mother is much more powerful and noble than that of all other relatives and friends. The mother is, therefore, held in high esteem all over the world. One may or may not respect others, but one must respect one's mother. A mother's love is always selfless. We should learn to cultivate such love. If you cannot win the love of your mother, how can you hope to win the grace of God? Hence, first and foremost you should strive to win the love of your mother.

Modern students do not try to win their mothers' love. The mother undergoes great ordeals; she is prepared to undertake even hard labour to earn a few rupees to bring up her children and educate them somehow. What a great sacrilege it will be to forget the love of such a noble mother! We are not born from the earth or the sky; we are born from the wombs of our mothers. It is possible that at times differences may arise between a mother and her son. But no mother would hate her son on that account; she would not forsake him. There may be sons who hate their mothers, but there are no mothers who hate their sons. The mother will always strive for the safety, health and welfare of her children.

People today are facing great difficulties because they are ignoring the love of their mothers. If you are able to win the love of your mother, you can win the love of all other people. The love of your mother will always be with you, constantly guarding and guiding you in all your endeavours. Unfortunately, people today do not realise this truth. They think, 'It is enough to provide a few morsels of food to that old lady'. They are so narrow-minded and selfish! It is a great mistake to think that their responsibility will end by providing some food to their mothers. The mother should be held in high esteem and served with love and devotion. She should be made to feel happy and contented.

There is no need for you to read voluminous books. Even a small book is good enough if it can help you to contemplate on God. Do not be satisfied with acquiring mere bookish knowledge. Such knowledge is only superficial. What you need really is the knowledge of the Self. Strive to acquire that knowledge. It manifests from within. It cannot be acquired from outside.

Is it not a fact that the more you dig the river bed, the more the water comes out of the sand? Similarly, the more you remove your bad thoughts, the more the sacred knowledge and sacred thoughts manifest in you. Purity, steadiness, wisdom and such other noble qualities are present in your heart. First and foremost, develop sacred thoughts. Do not bother about what others say about you. Do not leave your sacred path because of the adverse comments of others.

Try to develop faith in the truth that manifests from your own heart. It is not good to hate other castes and religions. Develop faith in your own religion and follow it diligently.

If you want you and your children to attain purity and sacredness, constantly contemplate on God. If the parents lead a good and noble life, their children will also be good and noble. Hence, the parents should be good in the first instance. Unfortunately, today the parents are unable to set an example to their children, with the result that the children are taking to bad ways. The parents should, therefore, sanctify their life by contemplating on God.

Many people ask me, 'Where is God?' I tell them, 'My dear! I am God; you are also God.' This is the truth. Why should we be afraid of speaking the truth? God resides in the heart of every being. All are the embodiments of God. There is divinity in every human being.

If one wishes to tread the path of devotion, one should hold firmly on to the principle of love. Ordinary mortals do not have such firm determination, but a true devotee of the Lord will never deviate from the path of love under any circumstances. No other path except love can take you to God. Develop love more and more. Love is with you, in you, around you. Love is changeless wherever you are; love is your sole refuge.

Let all your activities be suffused with love. Modern youth fail to understand the true meaning of love. Love cannot exist if there is a feeling of duality. Non-dual love is true love. A give-and-take relationship does not reflect the true spirit of love. One should keep giving and giving without expecting anything in return. That is true love. It is the sign of selfish love to desert someone in times of his difficulties. When you give up selfishness and strive for the welfare of others, only then can you have true love.

You should know the difference between matter and reality. Reality transcends matter. All is Brahman – God. Consider everything as divine and treat the dualities of life such as pain and pleasure, loss and gain with equanimity. One should remain unaffected by happiness and sorrow, gain and loss, victory and defeat. Never be carried away by the vagaries of the mind. When you go by the mind, you see only matter, since the mind is related to matter. Have no concern with matter. If you associate yourself with the mind, you cannot achieve non-duality. You can develop true love and devotion only when you give up duality.

Understand that the same principle of love exists in you and others. It is essential for every devotee to understand this principle of unity. Share your love with others without any expectation. Love everybody for the sake of love. When you extend your love to others, you can attain the state of non-dualism. The worldly love that you indulge in from morning to evening is not true love at all. True love is that which is focused on one form, one path and one goal. It is a great mistake to divide love and divert it to many directions. Love is God. God is love. Live in love. Only then can you realise the principle of oneness and attain fulfilment in life. You may choose any name you like, but you should chant it with love.

Your love should remain steady in pleasure and pain. Where there is love and devotion, there is no scope for differences. All differences are the making of your mind. Develop the feeling of oneness that you and I are one. Never think that you and I are different. When you give up the feeling of duality, you will attain unity and divinity. That is the sign of true devotion.

The principle of oneness cannot be explained in words; it has to be experienced through love. But you do not understand the true meaning of love, because you interpret it in the physical and worldly sense. Consequently, your love is never steady. It keeps changing. True love has no connection with the physical body. It should not be tainted with body attachment. The body is made up of matter. All that is related to matter will never give you peace and happiness. Hence, transcend the matter and see the reality. Develop the feeling of oneness. All are one, be alike to everyone. It is a big mistake to attribute worldly feelings to love.

Your names and forms are different, but the principle of love is the same in all of you. That is why I address you as the "embodiments of love". Love is always one, it should not be divided. Consider God as one and love Him wholeheartedly. Such one-pointed love towards God can be termed as true devotion.

Names and forms appear to be different, but the reality behind all these is one and the same. However, people are unable to look deep within themselves and experience this oneness. The power of love is unparalleled. There is no power greater than this. Love cannot be understood by experiments and investigations. It can be understood only through love and nothing else.

When you say "God, I will follow you", it means that God is separate from you. It is possible that you may lose your way. Hence you should pray, "God, please be with me always". In fact, He is always in you. When you enquire deeply, you will experience this truth. It is impossible to be away from Him. Many devotees proclaim, "Oh God, I am in You, I am with You and I am for You." They repeat these words in a superficial way; they do not say these words from the depth of their heart. Actually, God is never separate from you. Pray to Him wholeheartedly with firm conviction that He is always in you, with you, above you, below you and around you. When you offer such a prayer to God, He will certainly redeem your life.

Embodiments of Love! You have to understand that God is omnipresent. There is no place where you do not find God. The essence of the teachings of all scriptures is that God is present everywhere. Out of their ignorance, some people argue that God is limited to a particular place. Truly speaking, Divinity is present in everyone and is all-pervasive. This is the basic truth of all doctrines and philosophies. See everywhere God. If you see God everywhere, nothing bad will happen to you.

Some people call Him Rama, others adore Him as Krishna and still others worship Him as Buddha. Names and forms may vary, but God is One. God is not limited to a particular name, form, region or religion. There is only ONE God, who pervades every atom of the creation. Words fail to express the glory and grandeur of Divinity. People may describe Divinity in a number of ways, but no description can ever portray

Divinity in full measure. In fact, to describe Divinity is a sign of delusion. Where is God? You are all the embodiments of God. God pervades all beings as their life-breath. Such transcendental principle of Divinity cannot be described. One may do one's best to describe it at any length, yet all descriptions will fall short of what reality is.

Water is infinite; a container cannot hold more water than its capacity. As is the size of the container, so is the quantity of water collected. Likewise, God is infinite, but each one describes Him based on his limited understanding. Divinity is much more than a human mind can comprehend.

See no evil; see what is good,

Talk no evil; talk what is good,

Hear no evil; hear what is good,

Do no evil; do what is good,

Be always with God.

It is impossible for anyone to describe Divinity in full measure. God is one, but people may describe Him in various ways depending on their feelings. Divinity is one. It is a sign of ignorance to divide God in the name of religion and limit Him to a particular name and form. God is limitless and boundless. He is the all-knowing inner reality. God is present in everyone in the form of Atma (Spirit-Self). Develop such self-confidence and spirit of oneness.

People worship God by different names and forms, but God is One. The principle of the Atma (Spirit-Self) which resides in everyone is the true divine power.

Today many people practise meditation without knowing what it is. In the process, they waste a lot of time. What is meditation? Is it to sit cross-legged with closed eyes? No, not at all. People undertake meditation with deluded minds. Consequently they are unable to achieve the desired result. What is meant by meditation? To think of God at all times and under all circumstances is true meditation. You should install God in your heart and discharge your duties with the feeling that God is the basis of everything. Only then can you be called a true devotee of God.

Wherever you go, whatever you may do, recognise the truth that there is only one God and He is all-pervasive. Never give scope for differences saying, my God and your God.

Where is your God? Where is my God? All are one; be alike to everyone. There is ONLY ONE GOD and He is present in everyone.

It is sheer ignorance to say, "My God is different from your God." Those who quarrel with each other in the name of religion are foolish people.

It is a big mistake to think that God is different for different people. You should have firm faith that God is one.

When you develop such spirit of oneness, you will certainly have vision of the Divine. Everyone should develop spirit of oneness.

Maya (meaning illusion) is responsible for all delusion. Do not become a victim of Maya. When you cast aside Maya, then truth will manifest from within. When you transcend the senses, you see the dawn of consciousness. Truth is that which is close to consciousness.

Students should earn a good name in society and uphold the reputation and prestige of the institution in which they study. An educational institution is like a gigantic tree. Different subjects are like its branches and sub-branches. Virtues are like the fragrant flowers that you find on the tree. Faith is like the roots. When you water the roots of faith, you get the fruit of Ananda. Ananda means bliss.

Never eat food which can upset your stomach. When the food is pure, you will have pure thoughts and feelings. Pure thoughts make the mind pure and purity of mind makes a man noble. The people in Bharat (India) are aware of the impact of food on the mind. Even now there are many Indians who observe strict dietetic discipline and partake of pure food only. Many people occupying high positions are also now leaving the habit of eating non-vegetarian food.

The character of the students of an educational institution is of utmost importance. The end of education is character. Character is not limited to civilised behaviour and good conduct alone. One should consider fellow human beings as one's own brothers and sisters.

Love is the only means by which man can attain liberation. Many great souls reached their goal only through love. You should follow their example. Never lose your wealth of love. Make love as your primary objective in life. Love may appear to be very simple thing to you. But there is no power greater than love. God is love, love is God. Live in love. That is what you have to learn.

Education is not limited to mere reading of books. By reading books, we acquire the knowledge of many subjects. We should put this knowledge into practice and strive for God's grace. To attain God's grace, love is most important. Man can acquire great powers by love. It is by love alone that he can control the mind. He can even gain control over Nature through love. Spiritual practices also become fruitful by love alone.

The mind can never be controlled if you do not give up bad qualities, bad thoughts and bad company. Human nature can be sanctified only by divine and selfless love. Human beings are endowed with infinite love. The only property and power that will <u>never</u> diminish in the human being is love. You may share it with any number of people, yet it does not diminish; it will continue to grow. The reference in this context is not to worldly love, but to transcendental love. There is nothing in this world which can equal divine love.

Though we talk about divine love, we never try to possess it. Every individual, from the time he gets up till he goes to bed, must strive to make his life worthwhile by inculcating divine love. You must love your fellow human beings, treating them as your friends. The whole world can be united as a single family by cultivating such universal love. It is not possible by any other means. Therefore, develop universal love.

Dear students! You are struggling a lot to acquire education. By this education, you may perhaps secure a degree. But all this education is negative in character. You must acquire positive education which would bring out your latent qualities of love, peace, compassion, forbearance, sympathy, etc. You must cultivate these qualities by constant practice. If the human mind is to be transformed, it can be done only by love, nothing else. You know the nature of the mind. It is very strong and powerful. It cannot be controlled by any other way except love.

None can escape from the consequences of his actions. People may act as they please, but they cannot escape from the consequences of their actions. Whether one is an ignorant person or a noble soul, one has to face the results of one's actions. Let no one be under the illusion that he can commit sin and go scot-free. Hence, one should enquire before

performing an action whether it is good or bad. Wherever you go, the results of your actions will follow you like a shadow.

However, it is possible to mitigate the consequences of actions by the grace of God. God is always by your side, and is always blessing you by saying 'so may it be'! Humans are not realising this truth and are indulging in wicked deeds. They know pretty well what is good and what is bad, yet are unable to give up these evil ways.

All that man experiences in life is the result of his own actions, good or bad. You may think that you can commit a sin surreptitiously and feel that no one has seen you. But you cannot hide your actions from God. The consequences of your actions will follow you wherever you go. A person cannot be judged from his outward appearance. He may appear to be noble and great and speak in a pleasing manner, but his actions may not be compatible with his words. You may undertake any number of good deeds, but they cannot nullify the consequences of your past evil deeds. You have to bear this truth always in mind.

No one can comprehend the ways of God. They are inscrutable, mysterious and full of wonder. The principle of divinity is not visible to the naked eye, but it is this principle which makes you experience the fruits of actions.

You may not be able to comprehend fully all that is being said. But you will understand it when you experience it yourself. It is impossible to escape from Karma (fruits of actions). Sometimes, you may experience Karma later, much after the performance of the action. But you cannot escape from it. You may hide your action by saying that you have not committed any mistake. But you cannot do away with the action or the result thereof. You cannot cover up your sins forever. You read a number of books. But do you practise all that you have learnt? No no. You practise only that which is necessary and convenient for you. But there is no such option with regard to the results of your actions that you have once performed.

You may wonder if there is a way to escape from the consequences of Karma. Yes, it is possible for those who earn the grace of God. Once you become the recipient of God's grace, you will be saved from experiencing Karma. Hence, you should strive to earn God's grace. Scholars say, it is impossible to escape from Karma. What they say is true to a certain extent. But once you earn Divine grace, even if you have to experience the consequences of Karma, you will not feel the pain.

Just as the air is all-pervasive, God is present in you, with you, around you, below you and above you. Hence, you should be in communication with Divinity every day. When you have faith in Divinity, you will naturally have unity with God.

The world is full of mystery and wonder. It is nothing but the manifestation of five elements. It undergoes change with the passage of time. Likewise, the physical body which is also made up of five elements is subject to change. The ways of God are mysterious and beyond the grasp of human understanding. All that you see is not indeed the reality. In fact, human beings are incapable of fathoming the deep mysteries with their senses. It is not possible for anybody to hold on to the physical body forever. It remains so long as it is <u>destined</u> to be. It will perish at its predestined time. Nobody has any control over death. It is decided at the time of birth itself. The date of departure is imperceptibly written on the body when it comes into the world.

It is not possible for man to comprehend the way the universe functions. Who is responsible for the wonders and mysteries that we witness in this world? What one had to do, when, where and how, all this is predestined. Human beings have no control over it. Everything happens according to God's Will and His command. It is the primary duty of humans to obey the divine command implicitly. Everything in this world, perceptible or imperceptible, happens according to the Divine Will. One need not pay heed to what others say when it comes to obeying God's command. You have to obey the divine command in letter and spirit without adding any comma or full stop to it. Unfortunately, today nobody is making any real effort to understand the mysteries of God's creation.

Scientists boast of having unravelled the mysteries of creation, but they do not have true experience of the reality behind the phenomena of the universe. Each and every activity that takes place in this universe is full of wonder. When you observe carefully, you will be able to perceive the unseen hand of God at work everywhere.

God responds to the prayers of devotees and comes to their rescue when they have purity of heart.

The same principle of Atma (spirit – soul) is present in all beings. It is referred to as Easwaratwa (divinity). Divine incarnations such as Rama and Krishna can be recognised by their divine forms. Every incarnation has a particular form.

But divinity has no form. It represents the principle of truth that is present in all beings. It is responsible for creation, sustenance and dissolution.

Human beings are endowed with not one but three bodies – gross, subtle and causal. The physical form represents the gross aspect and can be seen. But the subtle body cannot be seen. It is the source from which our thoughts and words originate. The causal body represents our true nature. But the same principle of divinity is present at all the three levels.

Without thread, there can be no cloth. Without silver, there can be no plate. Without clay, pot cannot be made. Likewise, without Brahman (Divinity), there can be no world. Without the creator, there can be no creation. The Creator can be compared to thread and the creation to cloth. The Creator embodies all the three aspects – gross, subtle and causal.

When you contemplate on God, you should transcend the mind. By merely having thread, one cannot make cloth. Likewise, self-effort and divine grace, both are essential in order to achieve the goal of life.

Everyone can have the vision of the Atma (spirit – soul). All are endowed with such power. Enquire within yourself what you have achieved by reading a number of voluminous books. You have become hard-hearted. If this is the result of your education, why should you study at all? First of all, develop love. When you have love in you, everyone will become your friend. If your heart is not suffused with love, your life will become artificial. Life is meaningless without love.

The world appears to have innumerable names and forms. One should not get enmeshed in these names and forms. It is only when we transcend the names and forms and know the underlying source that it is possible for us to recognize the truth. And that truth is "That Thou Art". That is constant integrated awareness is Brahman (God). The awareness is that the Self is Brahman – God.

Sugar made out of sugar cane juice is the main ingredient for making various sweets. Though there are different varieties of sweets, sweetness is common in all of them. Similarly, God is the source and sustenance for the entire universe. Wherever you see, you will find the manifestation of God in ever so many forms. The forms are subject to change, and are illusory in nature. God alone is the eternal changeless principle.

Life is like a train journey; young children have a long way to go, but elders have to alight from the train pretty soon. You must learn to make your journey comfortable and happy. Do not carry heavy, unwanted luggage with you that will make the journey miserable. Do not indulge in fault-finding and picking quarrels with others. Do not desire to have the best things for yourselves only. Share with others around you the good things you are given. Anger, hatred, envy and jealousy are the heavy luggage that I ask you to avoid taking with you on the journey.

One who realises his true identity is an educated person in the real sense. People enquire, "Who are you?" "Who is he?" etc, but they do not ask, "Who am I?" Man may acquire encyclopaedic knowledge about everything in this world, but of what use is it if he does not know who he really is?"

When you harm others, you actually harm yourself. Victory and defeat are part of the game of life. When someone meets with failure in his endeavour, empathise with him. Do not criticise or blame others. Differences occur when you do not identify yourself with others.

Who are you? You think you are the body and mind. Mind is nothing but a bundle of desires. One day or the other you will have to give up all desires. Hence, do not identify yourself with the mind. Man's mind wavers from moment to moment like a monkey. You belong to mankind. So, you have to conduct yourself as a human being. Do not allow your mind to behave like a monkey.

In India, we cultivate paddy. However, we do not consume it in its raw form. We remove the husk covering the grain and refine it into rice. Your desires are like the husk covering the rice grain. You will be FREE from the cycle of birth and death once you give up all desires. Paddy becomes suitable for consumption only after it undergoes the process of refinement and becomes rice.

We construct temples to consecrate idols and worship them. Where does the idol come from? It is your own creation. You offer worship to the man-made idols but you are not prepared to worship the God in man. There is no point in merely worshipping idols if you do not realise your innate divinity.

Give up body consciousness and live in the constant awareness that you are God.

Everyone must respect and revere the principle of the Atma (Spirit-Soul) within.

See God in everyone. God is all-pervasive. You cannot say that God is confined to a particular place. There is no place where God does not exist. With hands, feet, eyes, head, mouth and ears pervading everything, God permeates the entire universe.

Whatever you have learnt here, share it with others. But sharing with others is also not enough; you should put your knowledge into practice and derive benefit therefrom. We prepare many delicious items at home and serve them to guests. Is it not necessary that we should also partake of them? Likewise, you should digest the Vedic knowledge you have acquired and also share it with others. All knowledge has originated from the Vedas. That is why the Vedas are extolled as Sarva Vijnana Sampatti (treasure chest of all knowledge). But unfortunately, we are not making proper use of this treasure.

You will experience bliss when you share your knowledge of the Vedas with others. The Vedas contain deep spiritual truths.

You think, you are a human being because you are endowed with human body, but the Atma that indwells all manifests your divinity. There are thousands of bulbs that have been put up for decoration. Their colour and wattage may differ, but the electric current in all of them is one and the same. Like the current that makes all the bulbs shine, the Atma present in all human beings makes them see, hear and work. But today human beings are caught in worldly affairs and they are ignoring spirituality. If you have spiritual vision, you will know that it is the same God who is present everywhere. Everything from earth to sky is nothing but God. Even this flower, this tumbler, this microphone and the tablecloth that you see here are all aspects of divinity. Divinity pervades each and everything in this universe. But you see differences due to your faulty vision.

Change is the nature of the five elements and not of God. There are only five elements in this universe; there is no sixth element.

You have a pure and sacred heart, but it gets covered by the clouds of your desires. Just as the sun and the moon are not visible to us when they are covered by clouds, we are unable to visualise our reality because of delusion. Man passes his childhood in play with his playmates. In youth, he is deluded by ego as he feels proud of his youth. As the end approaches, he regrets for not having attained peace of mind because he kept hankering after worldly pleasures.

Human beings invite troubles in life by their own defects. If they improve their conduct, their life will become free from troubles. So, first and foremost you should take to the path of righteousness.

# Chapter Three

# A THOUGHT FOR THE DAY

**1st January.** Man cannot claim any achievement, for all are but instruments in the hands of the Lord.

**2nd January.** Faith in yourself and faith in God - that is the secret of greatness.

**3rd January.** You need to offer only two things to God: pure love and selfless service.

**4th January.** Those who walk with God always reach their destination. God is Love, love is God.

**5th January.** Self (ego) lives by getting and forgetting but Love lives by giving and forgiving.

**6th January.** Love All – Serve All.

**7th January.** The more you judge, the less you love.

**8th January.** Reason can prevail only when arguments are advanced without the whipping up of sound.

**9th January**. Man is not born to go in quest of food. Man is born to go in quest of the soul.

**10th January**. Take the world as it is. Never expect it to conform to your needs and your standards.

**11th January**. Duty without love is deplorable. Duty with love is desirable. Love without Duty is divine.

**12th January**. The secret of happiness is not in doing what we like, but in liking what we have to do.

**13th January**. It is easy to conquer Anger through Love, Attachments through Reasoning, Falsehood through Truth, Bad through Good and Greed through Charity.

**14th January**. One's anger is one's greatest enemy and one's calmness is one's protection. One's joy is one's heaven and one's sorrow is one's hell.

**15th January**. The purpose of education is to learn how to live, not how to make a living.

**16th January**. Truth is the very basis of Righteousness (Right Action). Just as burning is the nature of fire. Truth and good character are your very life breath.

**17th January**. It is wrong to desist from the appropriate action, placing reliance on destiny. If you do, even destiny will slip out of your hands.

**18th January**. Do not discuss devotion with those who have none; It will lessen your own.

**19<sup>th</sup> January**. Man's inhumanity to Man expresses itself in the form of natural catastrophes, like earthquakes.

**20<sup>th</sup> January**. Each will come in his own way at his own pace, along the path God will reveal to him as his own.

**21<sup>st</sup> January**. There is no peace for the truly compassionate, for it is the compassionate who suffer the burden of the world's pain.

**22<sup>nd</sup> January**. Education without character, science without compassion and commerce without morality are useless and dangerous.

**23<sup>rd</sup> January**. Wasting things is wasting God.

**24<sup>th</sup> January**. Only the man who gives up his own self-interest, regards the happiness of others as his own happiness and devotes himself to their well-being is a truly selfless person.

**25<sup>th</sup> January**. It is the heart that reaches the goal. Follow the heart, for a pure heart seeks beyond the intellect – it gets inspired.

**26<sup>th</sup> January**. If you do not rise above the things of the World, they will rise above you.

**27<sup>th</sup> January**. The good-hearted man who professes no religion is the truly religious man.

**28<sup>th</sup> January**. Those who walk with God always reach their destination.

**29th January**. Children should grow in the awareness of Brotherhood of Man and Fatherhood of God.

**30th January**. God's power is the power of love.

**31st January**. If you think that God is outside, how will your prayer reach Him?

**1st February**. Unable to realise your innate divinity, you waste your time searching for God outside.

**2nd February**. There is no greater spiritual exercise than following the path of love.

**3rd February**. Face all problems with courage and fortitude.

**4th February**. Human birth is meant to experience divinity and not to crave for fleeting pleasures. The human body is a divine gift.

**5th February**. God is not stone-hearted. His heart is filled with compassion.

**6th February**. God will always help you in all your endeavors, be they physical, moral, worldly, religious or spiritual.

**7th February**. All that God teaches is for the benefit and welfare of humanity.

**8th February**. The feelings of one's heart are most important. They are true, steady, changeless and eternal.

**9<sup>th</sup> February**. When you have love in your heart, you do not need to worry about anything. God will always be with you, in you, around you and will look after you in all respects.

**10<sup>th</sup> February**. God is in every creature, so how can you give pain to any creature?

**11<sup>th</sup> February**. Develop Purity of Thoughts.

**12<sup>th</sup> February**. Acquire the Knowledge of the Self.

**13<sup>th</sup> February**. Cultivate good habits and live by them!

**14<sup>th</sup> February**. Do not eat non-vegetarian food.

**15<sup>th</sup> February**. Take care of your health.

**16<sup>th</sup> February**. Love is the Royal Path for every human being's liberation.

**17<sup>th</sup> February**. Attain God through Love.

**18<sup>th</sup> February**. Everything depends upon God's Grace.

**19<sup>th</sup> February**. Develop Deservedness to attain God's Grace.

**20<sup>th</sup> February**. Sai is always engaged in serving mankind.

**21<sup>st</sup> February**. One who realises non-duality is a real human being.

**22<sup>nd</sup> February**. Experience your innate Divinity.

**23rd February**. The body is made up of five elements and is bound to perish sooner or later, but the in-dweller has neither birth nor death. The in-dweller is verily God Himself.

**24th February**. A yogi is one who transcends body consciousness and realises his true identity.

**25th February**. You are a three-in-one entity – the one you think you are i.e., the body, the one others think you are, the mind, and the one you really are, the Atma (Spirit – Soul).

**26th February**. Do not get infected by envy. Envy is invariably accompanied by hatred. These two are twin villains. They are poisonous pests. They attack the very roots of one's personality.

**27th February**. God is present everywhere, but though God is omnipresent, He cannot be seen.

**28th February**. Human life is the manifestation of Divine power.

**29th February**. God is present in every being in the world. He is present in insects, birds and beasts.

**1st March**. One should contemplate on God at least twice a day, in the morning and in the evening. By doing so, the heart will become pure and peaceful.

**2nd March**. There is no one in this world in whose heart God does not dwell.

**3rd March**. Human beings undertake many spiritual practices to attain "purity of heart". Without attaining this purity, God cannot be realised.

**4th March**. Prayer to God is one of the most powerful spiritual practices to attain purity of heart.

**5th March**. Man is the reflection of Divinity.

**6th March**. God is one. Develop firm faith in this principle. Do not ever attribute duality to God. God is one, and only one.

**7th March**. Since we do not understand the real nature of divinity, we refer to certain individuals as father, mother, uncle, etc., keeping in view their physical forms and their relationship with us. If people are so deluded on the basis of physical relationships, they are bound to get confused about the real nature of divinity.

**8th March**. Eat good food, have good company, foster good thoughts.

**9th March**. Time is the fundamental factor of human life. Humans should realise its importance in their life. Don't waste time. Time waste is life waste.

**10th March**. One should undertake only those actions which are noble and worthwhile. Only then does human life become purposeful. In fact, the goal of life can be achieved only when we undertake good actions, foster good thoughts and adhere to good conduct.

**11<sup>th</sup> March**. Every action performed by man has a result. There will be a good result for a good action and a bad result for a bad action. This is the eternal law.

**12<sup>th</sup> March**. One should practise the five human values of Truth, Love, Right Action, Non-violence and Peace. If you practise the first four you will get peace!

**13<sup>th</sup> March**. We eat a variety of items as food to sustain the body. But no one is making an enquiry whether the food he eats is proper or not; whether it is beneficial for him or not. You should always eat Sattwic (pure) food. By having pure food, you will be able to cultivate pure thoughts and perform pure actions.

**14<sup>th</sup> March**. Keeping good company develops good qualities. It is the bad company and wrong food that are responsible for all your evil qualities. If you want to cultivate good qualities, you have to eat pure food and keep good company.

**15<sup>th</sup> March**. I often observe that youngsters today join bad company the moment they enter school or college and continue to move about in bad company. As a result, they cultivate bad qualities, resulting in bad behaviour. *Tell me your company, I shall tell you what you are.*

**16<sup>th</sup> March**. Never read bad books. Bad books generate bad thoughts.

**17<sup>th</sup> March**. You should not read all sorts of trash like cheap novels, stories, etc. Such trash will generate bad thoughts in you and pollute your mind. It is only the mind that is responsible for good and bad thoughts. That is why it is said "mind is the cause of bondage and liberation of man".

**18<sup>th</sup> March**. Many students today consider it a fashion to read cheap literature that is available at a low price, with the result that cheap thoughts and cheap behaviour are generated in them.

**19<sup>th</sup> March**. Desire breeds wishes. Wishes cause birth and also death. When human beings are devoid of desire, they need not go through birth and death. The next birth is the result of unfulfilled desires in this life and is determined by them. Those who have no trace of desire for material objects can achieve the awareness of the Atmic (Spirit-Soul) reality.

**20<sup>th</sup> March**. Consider truth as the basis of your life, follow the path of righteousness. Then the principle of love will manifest in you.

**21<sup>st</sup> March**. When you develop love, you will be successful in all your endeavours.

**22<sup>nd</sup> March**. Human birth is meant to attain peace and not to occupy positions of authority. One may have all types of wealth and comforts, but life has no meaning without peace.

**23<sup>rd</sup> March**. I always teach the principles of truth and love. If you practise truth and love in your daily life, that will make Me very happy.

**24<sup>th</sup> March**. There are many people in this world who are fabulously rich, highly educated and occupy positions of great authority. But, in what way is the world benefited by them? They turn away the beggar who comes to their doorstep for alms. They have no time to help the suffering humanity. Nobody seems to bother about the condition of the poor and the downtrodden.

**25<sup>th</sup> March**. Having been born as a human being, you should strive for the welfare of society.

**26<sup>th</sup> March**. Adhere to the principles of Truth and Righteousness in life. Only then will your conduct become ideal for others in society.

**27<sup>th</sup> March**. How can you expect to attain happiness and peace if you are not prepared to help your fellow human beings?

**28<sup>th</sup> March**. We must realise that we are born to experience our innate divinity and not merely to enjoy worldly pleasures.

**29<sup>th</sup> March**. One should realise that God is present in all beings. The spark of divinity is present in all.

**30<sup>th</sup> March**. Man is not a mere mortal. He is essentially divine. Jiva (individual soul) is negative and Deva (God) is positive. Both the positive and negative are required for the electric current to flow.

**31<sup>st</sup> March**. God assumes the form of a human in order to move among men and protect the world. God is present in everyone in the form of the Atma (Spirit – Soul).

**1<sup>st</sup> April**. Develop firm faith that God is in you.

**2nd April**. A pure heart, a cleansed mind, a God-filled consciousness, will all help you to listen to the voice of God within you.

**3rd April**. Develop truth and love and you need not even pray to Me and everything will be added to you unasked.

**4th April**. <u>Service</u> is the highest worship. Service is the worship you offer to the God in the heart of everyone.

**5th April**. Do not be carried away by what others say. Have God Firmly installed in your heart.

**6th April**. You should not follow the body which is like a water bubble or the mind which is like a mad monkey. You have to follow the Conscience or Atma principle.

**7th April**. Human life is very precious and valuable. It is very sacred and holy. It is a life worth living. Human beings are not recognizing the value of life; they are misusing it by immersing themselves in only worldly pleasures and sensual pleasures.

**8th April**. The worldly pleasures, the bodily pleasures are enjoyed even by the beasts and birds and animals. If humans only enjoy physical pleasures, what is the difference between human beings and animals?

**9th April**. At the lower level is the animal stage. In the middle is the human quality. At the top is Divinity. Human beings who are in the middle have to look upwards, they should not look downwards.

**10<sup>th</sup> April**. How can man attain divinity? You keep saying God and divinity, but to attain divinity you have to look upwards and give up the lower thoughts.

**11<sup>th</sup> April**. First and foremost, human beings must try to control their desires gradually. As long as the desires go on increasing and multiplying, the human qualities go on declining and decreasing.

**12<sup>th</sup> April**. As you go on developing detachment from the world, your divine attachment will increase.

**13<sup>th</sup> April**. There is too much talking. Spiritual energy will be wasted because of talking. Here is a small example: There is a radio. When you put on the radio and hear the sound, there is a waste of electrical power. The body is like the radio, the intellect is like a switch, talk is a sound, current is our energy. A lot of energy is being wasted because of talk.

**14<sup>th</sup> April**. Whatever work you do, think that it is Godly. That is real spiritual practice.

**15<sup>th</sup> April**. If you are doing the wrong thing your conscience is not satisfied.

**16<sup>th</sup> April**. The body is an instrument, it is an inert thing. The mind is also inert. The inner power is only the Atma, which is giving splendour, energy and power to everything.

**17<sup>th</sup> April**. The body, mind, senses and intellect are but instruments.

**18<sup>th</sup> April**. Less luggage, more comfort, makes travel a pleasure. Life is like a long journey. Desires are the luggage. If you reduce the luggage, your travel will be very comfortable. Human beings have too many desires! That is very bad. The more desires one has the more restlessness we develop. When one reduces the desires and attachments, one will get peace of mind.

**19<sup>th</sup> April**. Where there is confidence, there is love. Where there is love, there is peace. Where there is peace, there is truth. Where there is truth, there is bliss. Where there is bliss, there is God.

**20<sup>th</sup> April**. Bad thoughts, ego, jealousy, hatred, anger… all these are the bad qualities. When you remove the bad qualities, immortality is in your palm. That is very, very important.

**21<sup>st</sup> April**. Removal of immorality is the only way to immortality.

**22<sup>nd</sup> April**. Be always happy. Think that "I am God". You and God are one.

**23<sup>rd</sup> April**. Before birth, who is the son, who is the mother? All these relations are like passing clouds, they come and go like passing clouds. But divinity comes and grows.

**24<sup>th</sup> April**. God is within you. God is always with you, in you, around you, behind you, everywhere. That is real love.

**25<sup>th</sup> April**. You have to control the bad thoughts. You are the master, you are not the slave.

**26th April**. I don't want anything from you, only your Love.

**27th April**. Consider everyone as the embodiment of divinity. God is the mother and father of all.

**28th April**. Don't have too many connections. Only say what is necessary. Don't talk too much on the roads, it is not good. Other people mistake you thinking... If you are quiet that silence itself is God. In that silence you can develop your heart properly, you get expansion of love.

**29th April**. Life is nothing but a limited company. You have to live within the limits. Talk in a limited way, see in a limited way and eat in a limited way. If you are within the limits it is safe.

**30th April**. Bad thoughts, bad looking (sight), and bad doing (action) are only animal qualities and not human qualities. With bad thoughts, you cannot get human qualities. Don't say bad things, don't talk evil, and don't hurt anybody. Always be happy. Happiness is nothing but union with God.

**1st May**. What is the secret of happiness? The secret of happiness is not in doing what one likes but in liking what one has to do.

**2nd May**. Time is very important. Time waste is life waste, don't waste time.

**3rd May**. Patience is all the strength that man needs.

**4th May**. God is the ocean, you are the waves – realise this and be FREE!

**5<sup>th</sup> May**. Truth and Love form the essence of My message.

**6<sup>th</sup> May**. Develop faith in the Oneness of God.

**7<sup>th</sup> May**. Realise your innate Divinity.

**8<sup>th</sup> May**. Desires are the cause of man's delusion.

**9<sup>th</sup> May**. Truth and Righteousness are the foundation of true education.

**10<sup>th</sup> May**. Acquire education which develops your character.

**11<sup>th</sup> May**. Your company influences your thoughts and conduct.

**12<sup>th</sup> May**. Consider the suffering of others as your own. Do not do unto others what you do not want others to do unto you. Love is the basis of everything. Grow in love.

**13<sup>th</sup> May**. See God in your fellow human beings.

**14<sup>th</sup> May**. Develop the spirit of oneness.

**15<sup>th</sup> May**. Help Ever – Hurt Never. Hence always strive to help everybody.

**16<sup>th</sup> May**. God incarnates to transform mankind – humanity.

**17<sup>th</sup> May**. True education is that which dispels narrow-mindedness and promotes unity. It teaches mankind to live peacefully with his fellow human beings and establish peace in the world.

**18<sup>th</sup> May**. God loves everyone. He does not hate anyone. In fact, God does not know what anger, hatred and envy are. Unfortunately, such a loving God is being subjected to criticism by many people. God brings about transformation in the hearts of human beings. If you pray <u>sincerely</u>, you can also experience transformation. Note this important point: that within a short period of time, the entire world will come together and live in peace and unity.

**19<sup>th</sup> May**. Let us all move together, let us all grow together, Let us all stay united and grow in intelligence together, Let us live together with friendship and harmony.

**20<sup>th</sup> May**. Develop love more and more. Expand your love.

**21<sup>st</sup> May**. If the inner feelings are good, your speech and actions will also be good. The essence of all knowledge is Educare. Even though you may acquire a number of degrees, you cannot be called truly educated if you lack purity of heart.

**22<sup>nd</sup> May**. Realise the sacredness of human birth.

**23<sup>rd</sup> May**. The human form is a combination of five elements, namely, earth, water, fire, air and either (space). It is the divine power of the Atma-Soul which makes the five elements function.

**24<sup>th</sup> May**. One does not become a human being merely because one is endowed with a human form. It is the conduct and behavior that make one a real human being.

**25<sup>th</sup> May**. God is the source of <u>everything</u>.

**26<sup>th</sup> May**. Love unites all.

**27<sup>th</sup> May**. Good and bad lie in your mind; they are not outside. Hence, correct your feelings in the first instance. Get rid of all animals qualities so that humanness can blossom in you. If you notice even a trace of hatred in yourself, drive it away at once.

**28<sup>th</sup> May**. The world is the manifestation of Divine Love.

**29<sup>th</sup> May**. God pervades the Five Elements.

**30<sup>th</sup> May**. God is the eternal witness.

**31<sup>st</sup> May**. True happiness lies in Union with God.

**1<sup>st</sup> June**. Get rid of your evil qualities.

**2<sup>nd</sup> June**. Understand the Divine Principle of Unity.

**3<sup>rd</sup> June**. Realise your Divinity with faith and devotion.

**4<sup>th</sup> June**. Absolute purity or perfection is not beyond man's capacity.

**5<sup>th</sup> June**. I am aware of the past, present and future of every individual, irrespective of his caste, religion and place of birth. Some people who come here may think, "Perhaps Swami (another name for Sai Baba), does not know who I am." But, there is nothing that I do not know. Even though I know everything, I pretend as if I do not know.

**6<sup>th</sup> June**. Human being is a mixture of five components – body, mind, intellect, consciousness and senses. Since these five components are the very basis of his being, man has to keep them pure if he wants to proceed on the path of liberation.

**7<sup>th</sup> June.** All are the children of God.

**8<sup>th</sup> June.** Earn the Grace of God.

**9<sup>th</sup> June.** Do as you say. That is man's foremost duty. There should be perfect harmony between one's words and actions. On the other hand, if one says one thing and does something contrary to it, it connotes unrighteousness.

**10<sup>th</sup> June.** Atma (name given to our spirit – soul), is the nameless, formless Divinity.

**11<sup>th</sup> June.** Follow the path of truth and right action.

**12<sup>th</sup> June.** As you sow, so shall you reap.

**13<sup>th</sup> June.** World is Reaction, Reflection and Resound.

**14<sup>th</sup> June.** People think that it is God who is the cause of their happiness and sorrow. But it is not really so. Each one is responsible for his or her actions and reaps their consequences, good or bad. God is the eternal witness and does not interfere in this. If you talk endearingly to someone, he will also speak to you in the same loving manner. But if you talk in an arrogant way, you will get a similar response. As is the action, so is the reaction.

**15<sup>th</sup> June.** Be good, do good, see good.

**16<sup>th</sup> June.** You may think that you are highly educated and very intelligent. But how can you call yourself so if you are ignorant of your true Self?

**17<sup>th</sup> June.** When you gain control over your mind, everything else will come under your control. Therefore, you should make all efforts to control your mind. Then you are sure to become an ideal and great person.

**18<sup>th</sup> June.** Nurture and develop your innate qualities.

**19<sup>th</sup> June.** Lead an ideal and exemplary life.

**20<sup>th</sup> June.** First and foremost, develop sacred and selfless love. When people share their love with each other, the whole world will be replete with love. But do not taint your love by selfishness and self-interest.

**21<sup>st</sup> June.** A mother's love has immense power.

**22<sup>nd</sup> June.** Make sacred use of your senses. There is always a reward for our good deeds, whether we aspire for it or not. Likewise, we cannot escape from the dangerous consequences arising out of our seeing, thinking, hearing, talking and doing all that is bad.

**23<sup>rd</sup> June.** Love is the true human quality. Consider love as your very life-breath. One without love is no better than one without life.

**24<sup>th</sup> June.** Wherever you are, whatever may be the situation, never deviate from the path of love and truth. Do not try to distort truth in order to fulfill your desires.

**25th June**. Never use your senses in an unsacred manner. Today people are interested in seeing wrong things. They are all ears when someone indulges in vain gossip and evil talk. Never lend your ears to evil talk and get carried away by it.

**26th June**. Attain enlightenment by renouncing desires.

**27th June**. All the names and forms are but the manifestations of the Supreme Being who is Existence-Knowledge-Bliss Absolute and non-dual. He is the embodiment of Truth, Goodness, Beauty.

**28th June**. Recognize the Unity of all Creation. True wisdom lies in seeing oneness.

**29th June**. There are three lines along which endeavour have to be directed: (i) spiritual exercises and discipline, (ii) cultivation of detachment, (iii) development of confidence in one's Self. Without these three, life is a wearisome and wasteful journey. Give up, renounce – that is the virtue you need for spiritual progress. It is not the value of the thing given up that counts, it is the loftiness of the impulse behind the act.

**30th June**. On the one side is the world and on the other, God. You cannot have both simultaneously. It is like riding two horses, which is sure to prove dangerous. Focus your mind only on God and have total faith in Him.

**1st July**. The youth should follow the path of truth and right action.

**2nd July**. Acquire education that gives knowledge of the Self.

**3ʳᵈ July.** The individual should serve society. In fact, service to society is the most important duty of human beings. Service to society is, in reality, service to Divinity.

**4ᵗʰ July.** Since every being is a part of the Divine, all should be respected, loved and adored. You should not hate anybody and should not create distance between one another. Just as all the parts of the body form one organism, similarly all beings are like various limbs of God.

**5ᵗʰ July.** Your very form is love. It is love that protects the whole world. The five elements that constitute the universe are based on love. Only when love combines with the five elements does the universe come into existence.

**6ᵗʰ July.** The only thing that is permanent and eternal is Love.

**7ᵗʰ July.** You may earn any amount of money, but as long as you are alive you should give joy to others by undertaking acts of charity. Those who have money should look after the poor and sick people.

**8ᵗʰ July.** If you really want to see God, first see Him in everyone.

**9ᵗʰ July.** Humanness blossoms in a pure heart.

**10ᵗʰ July.** Face all difficulties with forbearance.

**11ᵗʰ July.** Fill your heart with love and not with the poison of evil qualities.

**12th July**. Atma (the spirit –soul part of you) has neither a form nor a name. Atma is referred to as Brahma (God). Brahman alone is real, the world is unreal.

**13th July**. God is present in your heart in the form of pure and unsullied love.

**14th July**. There is no weapon more powerful than love.

**15th July**. Treat each other with love, converse with each other with love, lead a life full of love and enjoy bliss.

**16th July**. Nothing is permanent in this World.

**17th July**. Man has a relationship with the five elements so long as the body lasts. Once the body perishes, he has nothing to do with even one of them. These elements are present in man in the form of his senses of sound, sight, touch, taste and smell. Our senses are responsible for good and bad, merit and sin. Good and bad are not given by God; they are the consequences of man's own actions.

**18th July**. You may come and go, but I am with you forever.

**19th July**. Everybody has to leave the world empty-handed.

**20th July**. Do all actions to please God.

**21st July**. All of you are the embodiments of love and divinity. For the sake of identity, you have name, but in reality, all of you are the embodiments of the Atma (the divine spirit). Only the Atma is eternal.

**22nd July**. Worry is a mentally created fear.

**23ʳᵈ July**. All that has to happen will happen. Do not worry about it. Past is past, forget the past. Future is uncertain, do not brood over it. Present is important, live in the present and be happy.

**24ᵗʰ July**. Hurry, worry, curry are the causes of heart diseases. One should therefore avoid hurry, worry, and curry.

**25ᵗʰ July**. Live always in Bliss.

**26ᵗʰ July**. Pray for the welfare of all. Pray Loka Samasta Sukhino Bhavantu which means *"May all the people in the world be happy!"*

**27ᵗʰ July**. God incarnates on Earth to re-establish Righteousness (Right Action).

**28ᵗʰ July**. One cannot attain the vision of God merely by doing worship, it is only by developing purity of heart and noble qualities, that one can have vision of God.

**29ᵗʰ July**. God is Omnipresent. He is the creator, sustainer and destroyer of all the objects and beings of the universe. Every object in this universe is a gift of God who is immanent in all of them. Hence, whatever object you observe, do not consider it merely inert matter; it is a form of divinity.

**30ᵗʰ July**. All that is related to God is good.

**31ˢᵗ July**. Good words result in good actions.

**1ˢᵗ August**. When your words are good, your heart will also be good. When your heart is full of sweetness, all your feelings will also become sweet. Therefore, make your heart pure, soft and sweet.

**2ⁿᵈ August**. Lead your lives with compassion, kindness nd love.

**3ʳᵈ August**. Goodness is not to be acquired from somewhere outside. It is inherent in your nature. You have only to develop it. Just as proper care and nourishment are required for a small sapling to grow into a gigantic tree, you have to make efforts to develop your goodness.

**4ᵗʰ August**. Ego is the cause of many evil qualities.

**5ᵗʰ August**. Come just one step forward towards Me and I shall take a hundred towards you.

**6ᵗʰ August**. Where there is faith, there is love; where there is love, there is truth; where there is truth, there is God.

**7ᵗʰ August**. You may doubt the fact of the omnipresence of God, but if your realise that your body is the temple of God, your own heart is the seat of God and that the consciousness in you is simply a reflection of God, then your meditation room is your body itself and so He is present wherever you go.

**8ᵗʰ August**. Wherever and whenever you think of Me, I shall be with you. Whenever you call to Me, I shall respond.

**9ᵗʰ August**. The calamity that has befallen mankind will be averted. A new Golden Age will occur. I shall not fail. It is not in the nature of Avatars to fail!

**10th August**. Life must be full of love. Love must manifest itself in everything you do in life and that means throughout the day.

**11th August**. Man's soul or human spirit is the indestructible Divine itself. It has come from God, it is part of God. God is the inner Reality of All Beings. The human body is a Gift from God to each one of you. I have come to light the lamp of love in your hearts.

**12th August**. God is the moving force in every person. He is behind all good impulses and all useful attributes. You are all separate beads that are strung together on one thread – GOD.

**13th August**. I do not come and go. I am everywhere present, at all times.

**14th August**. Man is not born to go in quest of food. Man is born to go in quest of the soul.

**15th August**. Good company fosters goodness – always keep good company.

**16th August**. Study well and achieve excellence in your studies. Along with this, develop good character and conduct.

**17th August**. Devotion to God will make your life Divine!

**18th August**. Make your life divine by developing devotion to God.

**19ᵗʰ August**. Man should realise his Divine Nature.

**20ᵗʰ August**. Divinity is all-pervading. There is no place in this universe which is not permeated by God. There is no object in this world which is not divine. One divine principle manifests itself in different forms.

**21ˢᵗ August**. Though divine consciousness is immanent in all beings, mankind is unable to realise it due to his body attachment. It is overshadowed by the body-mind-intellect-mind stuff-ego complex of man.

**22ⁿᵈ August**. A human being should lead his life in a manner that is worthy of his status of man. He should not allow himself to degenerate into an animal.

**23ʳᵈ August**. Lead your life with love. Do not hate anybody.

**24ᵗʰ August**. One who constantly contemplates on God is the noblest of all human beings.

**25ᵗʰ August**. You are embodiments of love. You cannot live without love even for a moment. You may express love in any form, but lead your life as an embodiment of love.

**26ᵗʰ August**. Always remain conscious of your Divinity.

**27ᵗʰ August**. Understand the difference between Truth and Illusion.

**28ᵗʰ August**. You consider everything that you see in this objective world as true. But, in reality, nothing is true in this world. Truth is that which is eternal, beyond the three periods of time – past, present and future. That is God.

**29th August**. All worldly relations are temporary.

**30th August**. Everything in this world is subject to change. It appears to be permanent, but it is not so. God is the only changeless principle.

**31st August**. At the time of his birth, man is pure and sacred. As he grows up, he gradually loses his purity. This is not proper.

**1st September**. Spiritual practice is necessary to attain purity.

**2nd September**. As long as people live in this world, they keep thinking about property and wealth only. They do not think about what will happen to them after death, which can occur anywhere at any time.

**3rd September**. It is God only who protects and sustains you. He is your father, mother and everything in life. Everything that you have is only by God's grace.

**4th September**. Give up selfishness and strive for self-realisation. Enquire "who am I?" Are you the body, mind, intellect, mind-stuff or ego? No, none of these. Recognise your reality "I am I." Understand this truth through proper enquiry.

**5th September**. There are numerous people with high degrees like M.A., M.B.A., and Ph.D. in this world. But what service are they rendering to society? They are concerned with furthering their own interests and are not bothered about helping others.

**6<sup>th</sup> September**. The real worth of education lies in self-sacrifice and selfless service.

**7<sup>th</sup> September**. Never become narrow-minded, be large-hearted!

**8<sup>th</sup> September**. Be in good company. Your company determines the type of person you are. If you join bad company, you will also become bad. Say goodbye to bad company and leave the place immediately where you find such a company.

**9<sup>th</sup> September**. Where is the cause for worry when God is there to take care of you?

**10<sup>th</sup> September**. Do not put undue burden of responsibilities on yourself.

**11<sup>th</sup> September**. Too many desires ruin human beings lives.

**12<sup>th</sup> September**. Today wherever we go, we find only craze for money. Even old people who are nearing the ends of their lives are crazy for money. Man today has too many desires.

**13<sup>th</sup> September**. We give too much importance to the body, which is like an iron safe. Instead, we should give more importance to the precious jewels of human values within. Values should be the prime concern of human life.

**14<sup>th</sup> September**. Without values, human life does not serve any purpose. Birds and animals have love in them, but they have no desires. They are contented when their hunger is satiated. But man is not like that. He wants everything and everything. If he owns five buildings, he wants ten more.

**15th September**. Today man has excessive desires. He has to reduce his desires. Less luggage more comfort makes travel a pleasure.

**16th September**. Once you can control your desires you can live in peace.

**17th September**. Never reduce your love for God. Develop more and more love for God, and then you will have everything.

**18th September**. Install the values of Truth, Right Action, Peace and Love in your heart permanently.

**19th September**. If you have peace and love, you can achieve anything in life.

**20th September**. If you ask our students, you will find that all of them have full control over their desires.

**21st September**. Wherever you look, you find people full of desires. What do they achieve by having too many desires? Ultimately, they ruin their life. So, it is necessary for you to control your desires. With heavy luggage on your head, how far can you walk? Reduce your luggage to make the journey of your life more comfortable.

**22nd September**. Treasure love in your heart. Love all. But do not unduly burden yourself with too many responsibilities. This will add to your worries and difficulties. You can lead a happy life only if you reduce your burden. Then there will be less scope for difficulties and suffering.

**23rd September**. Death is certain some day or the other. You have the body today, but you may not have it tomorrow. Therefore, earn a good name even at the cost of your life. Consider good name as your very life-breath. Good name will remain even after one departs from this world.

**24th September**. Share your love with everyone. Do not limit your love to your family only, leading a selfish life.

**25th September**. Duty is God. Work is worship. Follow these twin principles in life. Do not put undue burden of responsibilities on yourself.

**26th September**. Where is the cause for worry when God is there to take care of us?

**27th September**. Once you surrender everything to God, you should be free of worries. You can experience peace only when you are free of worries.

**28th September**. When you develop love for Paramatma (God), you can experience the joy of Prakriti (nature).

**29th September**. You may perform any number of spiritual practices but all these are useless if the inner meaning is not understood.

**30th September**. Man extols God as omnipresent (everywhere), omniscient (all knowing) and omnipotent (all powerful), but he ignores His Presence in himself!

**31st September**. Each religion forgets that God is all forms and all names, all attributes and all assertions.

**1st October**. There is only ONE religion, the religion of LOVE.

**2nd October**. I am the embodiment of love; love is MY instrument. There is no creature without love; the lowest loves itself, at least. And its Self is God.

**3rd October**. The path of love is the royal road that leads mankind to Me.

**4th October**. Any knowledge that is not put into practice is no knowledge at all. Put into practice one or two principles in your life out of all that you have learnt.

**5th October**. Instead of getting entangled in worldly life, you should engage yourself in the service of society.

**6th October**. Once you take to the path of service, your problems will gradually decrease. Love all, Serve all.

**7th October**. Do not consider anybody as another person. Develop the feeling that he and you are one. The whole of mankind is one.

**8th October**. There may be some ups and downs in life, but once you have surrendered to God, nothing will disturb you.

**9th October**. It is right action that leads man to peace. Without peace, human beings cannot live. Saint Thyagaraja said, "One cannot have happiness without peace". When you attain peace, you will experience love and bliss. Truth is the origin of bliss.

**10ᵗʰ October**. Non-violence also emerges from truth. A man of love will not entertain any thought of violence.

**11ᵗʰ October**. Truth, Righteousness, Peace, Love and Non-violence are like the five life-breaths of man. These are the prime qualities of a human being. The need of the hour is to develop these human values. Only when these values are developed can there be peace in the country.

**12ᵗʰ October**. Peace and Happiness lie in Spirituality and in nothing else.

**13ᵗʰ October**. First is the body. Next come the senses. Higher than the senses is the mind and the intellect is higher than the mind. The Atma (spirit – soul) is the highest. When you understand and contemplate on the principle of the Atma, you will be free from all suffering and bondage. It is the perversion of the mind that is the cause of all your sufferings and bondages.

**14ᵗʰ October**. You should work hard and make others happy.

**15ᵗʰ October**. You should study well and earn a good name in society.

**16ᵗʰ October**. When you make your mother, father, preceptor and guest happy, then God will give you more happiness.

**17ᵗʰ October**. You may study, get married, have children and lead a happy life. There is nothing wrong in it. But never forget God.

**18ᵗʰ October**. Spread the Divine Name in every nook and corner of the world. That will lead to manifestation of divinity within everyone.

**19ᵗʰ October**. Worldly pleasures are no pleasures in the real sense of the term. Today you may have pleasure, tomorrow you may experience pain.

**20ᵗʰ October**. Nowadays, learning is limited only to physical and worldly aspects; moral, ethical and spiritual aspects are left out.

**21ˢᵗ October**. Never give room for evil qualities like anger, hatred and jealousy.

**22ⁿᵈ October**. We should develop the five human values of Truth, Righteousness, Love, Non-violence and Peace, which will promote harmony and unity in the world.

**23ʳᵈ October**. We should develop those qualities which will bring us closer to each other and not the ones which will distance us from each other.

**24ᵗʰ October**. You are all sparks of divinity. You are not mere mortals. You are not separate from God.

**25ᵗʰ October**. Do not waste your time in vain gossip.

**26ᵗʰ October**. Consider all your fellow men as your brothers and sisters and strengthen the bond of love with them.

**27ᵗʰ October**. Today man runs after all that is perishable, ignoring that which is immortal.

**28th October.** That Thou Art – this profound statement of the Vedas contains the essence of all knowledge. You are God.

**29th October.** Practise of human values promotes Unity and Harmony.

**30th October.** All that human beings experience are the result of their actions.

**31st October.** Leave the burden of all your responsibilities to God.

**1st November.** I am always happy. You should also always be happy. Happiness is union with God.

**2nd November.** The root cause of man's ill-health today is bad food and impure water. All that we consume must always be pure and sacred.

**3rd November.** We should take daily baths, eat good food and have sound sleep. Only then can we lead a happy life.

**4th November.** One can observe that those who eat good food, drink clean water and breathe unpolluted air are always healthy.

**5th November.** Man's thoughts are the root cause of his sickness. Hence, we should always have good thoughts.

**6th November.** Worries do not affect you when you contemplate on God.

**7th November.** Our Karmas (actions) are responsible for the happiness and sorrow we experience in life. When we perform good actions, we get good results. Bad actions have bad results.

**8th November**. Cultivate good thoughts and undertake good actions. Be good, do good and see good. This is the way to God.

**9th November**. Sorrows, difficulties and pain can come nowhere near Me. I am always happy and blissful. Bliss is My food.

**10th November**. I expect that you should face difficulties with courage, reposing faith in God.

**11th November**. If you constantly contemplate on God, no other thoughts will trouble you. Sorrows and difficulties will not affect you.

**12th November**. I am always happy. You should also always be happy.

**13th November**. When you are in union with God, you will not feel any pain or suffering. You may have some physical pain or mental anxiety, but if you are firmly established in the principle of the Self, you will not be bothered by them. (Authors Note: When speaking of the Self, He means believing in the fact that you are part of the Divine Spirit).

**14th November**. Happiness is union with God.

**15th November**. Consider sorrows and difficulties as 'passing clouds'.

**16th November**. Today human beings live a life full of desire, anger and ego.

**17th November**. All that we see and experience in this world is unreal and impermanent. Only God is real and true.

**18th November**. Cultivate good conduct. Then, everything will turn out to be good for you.

**19th November**. It is only when you are able to satisfy your conscience that you will be happy, peaceful and contented in life.

**20th November**. The physical, mental and intellectual power of youth is matchless. If they take a firm resolve, they can achieve anything. They should utilise all their powers for the benefit of society. Unfortunately, today's youth are becoming weak by succumbing to trivial attractions.

**21st November**. The youth of today are wasting money, food and time.

**22nd November**. Your life is a gift from your parents. Hence, you should love your parents wholeheartedly under all circumstances.

**23rd November**. Realise the intimate relationship that exists between the individual and society and promote the welfare of society.

**24th November**. God is always with you, in you, around you.

**25th November**. Truth is inside.

**26ᵗʰ November**. You have to love and respect others, then you will receive their love and respect.

**27ᵗʰ November**. The mind is the witness of the mind, virtue is the witness of virtue, and a fool is the witness of all foolishness.

**28ᵗʰ November**. Tell me your company, I shall tell you what you are. As is your company, so you become.

**29ᵗʰ November**. You are nuggets of gold. However, you should not be like 14 carat gold, you should be like 24 carat gold. Do not lose your value.

**30ᵗʰ November**. You should not impart merely physical and worldly education to children. You should also expose them to moral, ethical and spiritual knowledge. Infuse self-confidence in students.

**1ˢᵗ December**. Make students shining ideals of goodness.

**2ⁿᵈ December**. Make every effort to inculcate goodness in children in spite of all your difficulties and problems. That is your primary duty. Teachers are the true leaders of the country, not the political leaders.

**3ʳᵈ December**. Make children shining ideals so that their light of goodness spreads to every street and village, giving joy to one and all.

**4ᵗʰ December**. Money cannot bring real happiness. Human beings can attain happiness only through right conduct, sacrifice and love.

**5th December.** We are not born into this world to eat, drink and sleep. Lord Krishna declared that the eternal Atma (soul) in all beings is a part of My Being. Each being is an aspect of divinity. Not only human beings but birds, animals and insects are also embodiments of divinity.

**6th December.** All are embodiments of divinity.

**7th December.** Love is your true nature. Having been blessed with human birth, you should lead your life with purity of thought and action.

**8th December.** Man today is beset with so many worries. You cannot carry on your life if you are bogged down by worries. Never give scope to worry; lead a life full of happiness.

**9th December.** If you sow the seeds of truth, righteousness, peace, love and non-violence in children, they will set not only this country but the entire world on the right path.

**10th December.** Rest is essential for the human body. Therefore, every human being should take sufficient rest.

**11th December.** One should not stay awake at night for a long time; one should have sound sleep.

**12th December.** Never tell a lie. Do not resort to injustice or unlawful acts.

**13th December.** Attain immortality by following the path of truth. You are an aspect of the Divine. You should never forget this truth. Whatever study you may undertake, keep this truth always in your mind.

**14ᵗʰ December**. There is only one religion, the religion of Love. Religion means Love.

**15ᵗʰ December**. Do not turn a deaf ear to the words of your elders. If you put their advice into practice, then everything good will happen to you. Today nobody listens to the wholesome advice given by elders.

**16ᵗʰ December**. When you associate with good people, you will also become good. Who are your friends? Only good people are your true friends. You become like those whom you associate yourself with.

**17ᵗʰ December**. You should always have good character. Love and respect everyone. Never hate anybody. Earn a good name. It is our educational qualifications that confer greatness on us.

**18ᵗʰ December**. God is immanent in everyone. Names and forms may be different, but God is only one. He is present in all of you. All of you are the embodiments of Divinity. Develop this strong conviction.

**19ᵗʰ December**. Lead your life with the firm faith in the Brotherhood of Man and Fatherhood of God.

**20ᵗʰ December**. My acts are evidences of Divine power, signs and signals of Divinity. I am granting things out of Prema (love). My love will never diminish. I have no desire of any kind. I talk of love; I guide you along the path of love. I am Love.

**21st December**. Man can liberate himself only by knowing himself. He may master the universe, but what can he claim to have known when he has not mastered himself?

**22nd December**. Truth, righteousness, peace, love and non-violence are the five human values to be cultivated by a human being. You should learn all about these human values and put them into practice.

**23rd December**. There are no blemishes in human beings; they are the embodiments of love. But at times, some bad qualities like anger, hatred, jealousy, ostentation, etc., overpower them.

**24th December**. Love all, serve all. If you have love, you can achieve anything. Love is everything. Love is life; life is love. Life should be filled with love, not hatred.

**25th December**. A human being should speak softly, sweetly and lovingly.

**26th December**. When your conduct and speech are bad, how can you have peace? Peace is not to be found outside; it is within you.

**27th December**. You keep saying "I want peace, I want peace, I want peace." Let your conduct be good. Then, peace will flow from within you.

**28th December**. A millionaire can build many bungalows, purchase any number of cars and have all conveniences of life. But if you ask him, he will say that he has no peace. Of what use is all this wealth, comforts and conveniences if one has no mental peace?

**29th December**. Do not think that God is somewhere away from you. He is always in you, with you, around you. Hold on to this truth firmly and lead a happy life. When you are alone, think "God is with me." Have firm faith, "I am not alone; both God and I are together."

**30th December**. Love unites All.

**31st December**. My Mission Is To Spread Happiness'. I do not take anything from anyone, except their Love and Devotion'.

Love and Faith are the cardinal principles for redeeming human life. My Life is My Message. I love everyone; that is My very nature. All are Mine whether they call Me by this name or any other name or even by no name! Divinity is the primal source of universal love. Faith in Divinity is the key to develop such love. The way of love alone can transform man and hence the world.

*THE END*